BRADSHAW'S GUIDE TO THE RAILWAYS OF IRELAND

Volume Eight

John Christopher and
Campbell McCutcheon

AMBERLEY

Left: Locomotive No. 74 at the Cashel (Cahir) railway station, at the foot of the Rock of Cashel, south Tipperary. See page 36. *(National Library of Ireland/wiki)*

About this book

This book is intended to encourage the reader to explore many aspects of the railways of Ireland. Through Bradshaw's account and the supportive images and information it describes the history of the railways, their engineering works, architecture and some of the many changes that have occurred over the years. Hopefully it will encourage you to delve a little deeper when exploring the railways and other works, but please note that public access and photography are sometimes restricted for reasons of safety and security.

First published 2015

Amberley Publishing
The Hill, Stroud
Gloucestershire, GL5 4EP

www.amberley-books.com

ISBN 978-1-4456-3866-9 (PRINT)
ISBN 978-1-4456-3883-6 (E-BOOK)

British Library Cataloguing in Publication Data.
A catalogue record for this book is available from the British Library.

Typeset in 9.5pt on 12pt Celeste.
Typesetting by Amberley Publishing.
Printed in the UK.

Bradshaw in Ireland

The liberality of English tourists has accustomed almost all the poor people of the country to expect pennies and sixpences; and every now and then, in the traveller's progress through the gap, a little urchin, plump and good humoured, though shame-fully ragged, will pop up at the road side, and ask for 'a penny to buy a book!' or offer a tastefully made bouquet of heather and wild flowers to ensure the loose coppers or small coin of the Sassenagh.

When reading Bradshaw's guide there is no doubt that he found much to admire on his travels in Ireland, in particular the beautiful lakes of the south-west, but this extract is a stark reminder that in the mid-nineteenth century this was a country under British rule, one to be regarded by the Victorian reader as their modern equivalent might view today's Third World destinations. Nonetheless, his writings remain as a fascinating time capsule from the earliest days of the railway and the emergence of that new breed of travellers, the tourists.

This is the eighth volume in the Amberley series of books based on *Bradshaw's Descriptive Railway Hand-Book of Great Britain and Ireland*, which was originally published in 1863. It is also the first to venture beyond the UK mainland.

As a young man George Bradshaw had been apprenticed to an engraver in Manchester in 1820, and after a spell in Belfast he returned to Manchester to set

Below: No. 107, a coupled 0-6-0, at Valencia harbour station on the Great Southern & Western Railway. This was a packet station for transatlantic liners. *(National Library of Ireland/wiki)*

George Bradshaw and the men of iron

As with the great Victorian engineers, George Bradshaw's fame and prosperity grew with the rapid spread of the railways. Bradshaw, Brunel and Robert Stephenson were close contemporaries – they were born and also died only a few years apart – although there is no record of Bradshaw, shown left, having met either of the engineers.

Below: *Punch*'s take on the ubiquitous Bradshaw guides and timetables.

THE FIRST "BRADSHAW"
A reminiscence of Whitsun Holidays in Ancient Egypt.   From an old-time tabl(e)ature

up his own business as an engraver and printer specialising principally in maps. In October 1839, he produced the world's first compilation of railway timetables. Entitled *Bradshaw's Railway Time Tables and Assistant to Railway Travelling*, the slender cloth-bound volume sold for sixpence. By 1840 the title had changed to *Bradshaw's Railway Companion* and the price doubled to one shilling. It then evolved into a monthly publication with the price reduced to the original and more affordable sixpence.

George Bradshaw died in 1853, but the company continued to produce the monthly guides and in 1863 it launched *Bradshaw's Descriptive Railway Hand-Book of Great Britain and Ireland* (which forms the basis of this series of books). It was originally published in four sections as proper guidebooks without any of the timetable information of the monthly publications. Universally referred to simply as 'Bradshaw's Guide', it is this guidebook that features in Michael Portillo's *Great British Railway Journeys*, and as a result of its exposure to a new audience the book found itself catapulted into the best-seller list almost 150 years after it was originally published.

Bradshaw's railways

Although Bradshaw's guides were aimed at the general traveller and not written from an engineering perspective, they were published at a time when the great engineers had driven the railways, with their cuttings, embankments and tunnels, through a predominantly rural landscape. It is fair to say that the railways are the Victorians' greatest legacy to the twentieth and twenty-first centuries. They shrank space and time. Before their coming different parts of the country had existed in local time based on the position of the sun, with Bristol, for example, running ten minutes behind London. The Great Western Railway changed all that in 1840, when it applied synchronised railway time throughout its area. The presence of the railways defined the shape and development of many of our towns and cities, they altered the distribution of the population and forever changed the fundamental patterns of our lives. For many millions of Britons the daily business of where they live and work, and how they travel between the two, is defined by the network of iron rails laid down nearly two centuries ago by the engineers and an anonymous army of Irish navvies.

The timing of the publication of Bradshaw's guides is interesting. This particular account is taken from the 1863 edition of the handbook although, for practical reasons, it must have been written slightly earlier, probably between 1860 and 1862. By this stage the railways had lost their pioneering status, and with the heady days of the railway mania of the 1840s over they were settling into the daily business of transporting people and goods. Having said that, the growth of the Irish railways ran a little behind those on the mainland. By the early 1860s the main network of railways within Ireland had been established, although, as we will see, some lines had yet to be built. Ireland's first railway, the Dublin & Kingstown Railway, had opened in 1834 and from the beginning the Irish railways were built to carry passengers rather than goods for the most part. There was neither heavy mineral traffic nor a large

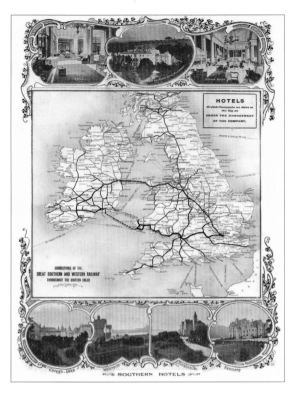

Above left: Cover of a guide book published by the Great Southern Railways in 1935. *Above right*: GSR route map published in *The Sunny Side of Ireland* in 1902. *Below*: The Great Southern & Western and the Midland Great Western display at the Palace of Engineering in the Wembley Exhibition held in London in 1924.

quantity of manufactured goods to be transported and the major coastal cities and towns could rely upon transportation by ship or boat.

By the early twentieth century Ireland's railways had been whittled down to four principal companies; the Great Southern Railways, the Great Northern Railway (Ireland), the Northern Counties Committee (London Midland & Scottish Railway), and the Belfast & County Down Railway. These were mostly to the 5-foot 3-inch gauge, as opposed to the British standard gauge of 4 feet 8½ inches, which was decided on by a Royal Commission to do away with the mishmash of gauges on the early lines. The Dublin & Kingstown Railway, for instance, was originally built to 4 feet 8½ inches, while the Ulster Railway had a wider 6 feet 2 inches, and the Dublin & Drogheda's rails were 5 feet 3 inches apart. Those entirely within the Irish Free State, the area covered in this volume, were combined on 1 January 1925 into the Great Southern Railways. This was the largest railway in Ireland and its route mileage was more than three times that of the others.

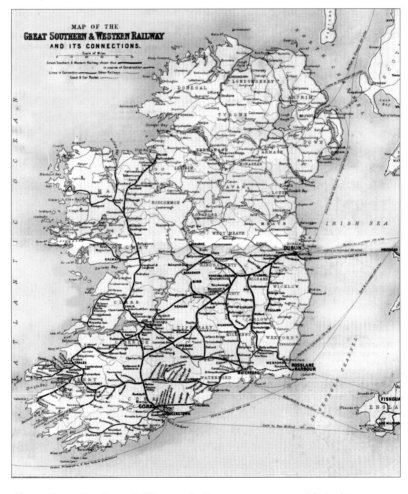

Above: Great Southern & Western Railway route map, published in 1902.

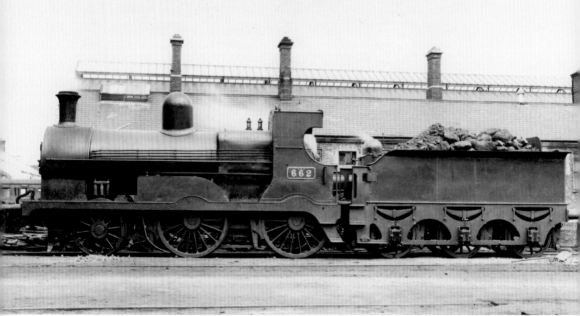

Top: GS&WR No. 200, a 6-0-0 of the J15 class. *Bottom*: No. 662, at the Inchicore Railway Works. Established in 1844 by the Great Southern & Western Railways, this is still the headquarters for mechanical engineering and rolling stock maintenance for Iarnrod Éiremann.

The guide

Without a doubt the Bradshaw Guides were invaluable in their time and they provide the modern-day reader with a fascinating insight into the mid-Victorian rail traveller's experience. In 1865 *Punch* had praised Bradshaw's publications, stating that 'seldom has the gigantic intellect of man been employed upon a work of greater utility'. Having said that, the usual facsimile editions available nowadays don't make especially easy reading with their columns of close-set type. There are scarcely any illustrations for a start, and attempts to trace linear journeys from A to B are interrupted by distracting branch line diversions. That's where this volume comes into its own. *Bradshaw's Guide to Ireland* takes the reader on a a series of journeys, starting with the Dublin to Cork and Killarney lines, with the branch to the south through carlow, Kilkenny and Waterford, and north to Limerick, and also the Midland Great Western line from Dublin to Mullingar, Athlone and Galway, as well as from Mullingar to Sligo. The final journey is northwards from Dublin on the line over the River Boyne on the Drogheda viaduct and upwards across the border towards Belfast with the final section covering Northern Ireland.

Bradshaw's writing on Ireland is not restricted to the practicalities of travel or the undeniable beauty of the great castles and lakes. Unusually, he makes several observations on the living conditions endured by many. In the section on County Tipperary he comments:

> It contains some of the most productive districts in the county; the peasantry, however, are the most riotous, distressed and poverty stricken. Trade and manufacture are scarcely known out of the large towns.

And later on his travels he contrasts the living conditions of the poor with those of the gentry. This concerns the county of Meath, to the north of Dublin:

> The farms are often very extensive, but the farm houses, except when they belong to large properties, are in general wretched huts; and the houses of the humbler classes are nothing but mud hovels. Yet the mansions of the nobility and gentry are numerous throughout every district, and in several instances are spacious and splendid.

So while Bradshaw's travelogue can be enjoyed as a nostalgic journey through nineteenth-century Ireland, this is still very much a product of its time. It was published less than twenty years after the Great Irish Famine (1845–1849) resulted in the deaths of a million people and saw the emigration of a million more.

The illustrations in this volume show scenes from Victorian times and later, and in many cases they are juxtaposed with modern photographs of the locations as they are today. The accompanying information provides greater background detail on the railways and the many locations along the route. Please note that Bradshaw's place names and spellings have been preserved as they appeared in the original 1863 text.

HOLYHEAD STATION.
PASSENGERS EMBARKING FOR DUBLIN. (NORTH WALL)

Left: Dockside station, Holyhead. The Chester & Holyhead Railway was built to enable Irish Mail trains to travel from London, via the West Coast Main Line, across north Wales to connect with the steam packets.

TO IRELAND VIA HOLYHEAD

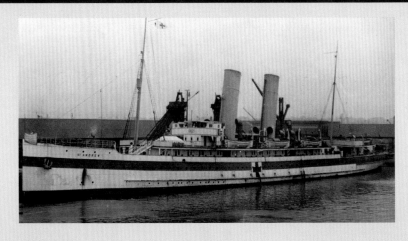

Above: Advertising card for the Holyhead service.

Left: The SS *St Andrew* was built for the Fishguard service of the Great Western Railway. During the First World War, it was used as a hospital ship.

Bradshaw's Ireland

Holyhead to Dublin

The passage across from Holyhead to Kingstown, a distance of 64 miles, is now generally performed in four to six hours, and the traveller has scarcely lost sight of the mountains of Carnarvon before those of Dublin and Wicklow become visible.

The entrance into the bay of Dublin unfolds one of the finest land and sea prospects ever beheld. On the right is the rugged hill of Howth, with its rocky bays, wanting only a volcano to render the surrounding scenery a facsimile of the beautiful bay of Naples; whilst, nearer to the eye, at the extremity of a white line of masonry just fringing the sea, the light-house presents its alabaster front. On the left are the town of *Dalkey*, with its romantic rocks, mutilated castles, Martello towers, elegant villas, and the picturesque town of *Dunleary*, whilst behind is seen a line of parks and plantations, above which the mountains of Wicklow ascend with the greatest majesty.

In the immediate neighbourhood of Kingstown, on the west side, are many excellent bathing-places. The sea here is singularly adapted for bathing. The sands are perfectly level; at least the eye cannot discern any declivity for a mile. When the tide is full, all these sands are covered to the depth of from two to three feet: when it is ebb-tide they are quite dry.

THE COUNTY OF DUBLIN, which returns two members, has its western limits formed by the Irish Sea, and the coast is rendered extremely picturesque in many parts by the bays and creeks into which it is broken. On the north and north-west it is bounded by the county of Meath. Part of the western border joins the county of Kildare, and, in the south, lie the mountainous tracts of Wicklow. Except in the attractive varieties of its coasts, and the beauty of the mountainous district which borders the county of Wicklow, this county may be considered as possessing less diversity of natural scenery than many other parts of Ireland.

KINGSTOWN

A telegraph station.

HOTEL – Rathbones. Rates of Porterage – 1s to 1s 6d for a quantity of luggage; 6d for a portmanteau and hat-case.

MARKET DAY – Saturday. REGATTA – In August.

Kingstown to Dublin

After traversing the Dublin & Kingstown railway, and stopping at the stations of SALTHILL, BLACKROCK, BOOTERSTOWN, and MERRION, we arrive at...

Above: The Dublin &
Kingstown Railway,
Ireland's first, had
opened in 1834.

Left: Cleaning Class F6
loco No. 46 in the Great
Western Railways shed
at Broadstone. *(National
Library of Ireland/wiki)*

Below: The imposing
Bank of Ireland building
on College Green, Dublin,
c. 1895. *(LoC)*

A telegraph station.

HOTELS – Bilton, 56, Upper Sackville Street, Lewis Heinkey; Reynolds', 12, Upper Sackville Street, F. Reynolds; Tuthill's, 51, Dawson Street, William Tuthill; Morrison's, 1, Dawson Street, John Baker; for Families. Commercial Buildings, 11, College Green, Henry Baker; Commercial, 23, Suffolk Street, B. Saunders; Wynn's, 35 and 36 Abbey Street, Mrs Pascoe; Commercial Hotels. Shelborne, Stephen's Green, Martin Burke; Gresham, 21 and 22, Upper Sackville Street, John Radley; Imperial, 21 and 22, Lower Sackville Street, James O'Toole (manager); Prince of Wales, 31, Lower. Sackville Street – Macken's, 12, Dawson Street, John Ennis; Hibernian, 48, Dawson Street, George Nesbitt; Anderson's, 32 and 33, College Green, Spadaccini; Jury's, 7 and 8, College Green, William Jury; Family and Commercial Hotels.

RAILWAY STATIONS – Galway, or Great Western, near the Queen's Inns and Broadstone Harbour; Drogheda and Belfast, near the Custom House and the Galway line; Great Southern and Western, or Cork line, King's Bridge, a fine granite front; Kingstown, in Westland Row; Wicklow, in Harcourt Road. The Irish gauge is 5¼ feet.

MARKET DAYS – Monday and Thursday, for cattle and sheep; Tuesday and Saturday for hay, etc.

DUBLIN, the capital of Ireland, and the second city of the British Islands, on the Liffey (*dew lin*, or 'black stream' in Irish), near Dublin Bay, 60 miles from Holyhead, and 292 miles from London. Population, about 254,850. Two members of parliament for the city, and two more for the university. It is about 3 miles in diameter and 11 miles in circuit. The appearance of Dublin is very much improved of late years. Streets have been widened, new squares skilfully laid out, and many public monuments freed from buildings which concealed their beauties. The police is also better attended to, and commercial activity seems to have revived. But the most beautiful spectacle that can be presented to the eye of a stranger is the vast panorama which suddenly opens itself on Carlisle Bridge. In front lies the magnificent Sackville Street, with its monument, splendid hotels, and the column erected in honour of Nelson; on the left the fine quays of granite, with their handsome balustrade, which bound for several miles the dark waters of the Liffey; on the right, and almost within the reach of the observer, thousands of masts rise between the banks of the river, between two ranges of lofty houses, and, at the foot of that admirable building which, with its majestic portico, elegant colonnade, pavement of marble, and dome of bronze, more resembles a noble Venetian palace than a prosaic Custom House. From the heights of the Phoenix Park one also enjoys a splendid prospect. In the midst of a vast lawn rises the palace of the Viceroy, surrounded by a treble fringe of shrubs and exotic plants. In turning the vides towards the Liffey, the prospect embraces the heavy masses of the old city, with

Kingsbridge station
Inset: This was the main Dublin terminus of the Great Southern Railways. *Main picture*:
GSR passenger train, hauled by a 4-4-0 express loco, shown shortly after departure from
Kingsbridge. Colour illustration from *Railway Wonders of the World*.

its steeples and towers, the Hospital of Invalids, and the high mountains in the distance which enclose, as with a girdle, the county of Dublin.

Except Irish poplius and coaches (at Hutton's factory), the manufactures are of no consequence; but the shipping trade is important and increasing, the port having been so much improved that large ships can come up to the quays which line both sides of the river. The tonnage belonging to the port is about 45,000, and the total customs 1¼ million; wine being a staple article of import. Guinness's stout, and Kinahan's L. L. (or Lord Lieutenant's) whisky, are both noted. A long sea wall and pier of three miles runs to Poolbeg lighthouse, commanding a view of the beautiful bay, which is 6 miles across, with a sweep of 15 or 16 miles; but the best points for viewing it are from the Hill of Howth (500 feet high), and Killiney Hill (470 feet), at the north and south extremities, looking down on the city, on Dalkey Island, Kingstown harbour, Blackrock bathing-place, and Clontarf, where Brian Boru beat the Danes (1014). Another view from Dunsink observatory. Perhaps the best view of Dublin is that from Carlisle Bridge, which embraces Sackville Street, the Nelson Pillar, the Four Courts, Custom House, Post Office, the Bank, and University on College Green. It contains many large and splendid buildings, but our limits prevent us from giving more than a list of the most striking. The eastern half is the newest and best built.

PUBLIC BUILDINGS – The *Bank* is the most perfect building in Dublin, built in 1739, for the Irish parliament, in the Ionic style, 147 feet long. The old House of Peers has the Battle of the Boyne worked in tapestry, and Bacon's statue of George III, and the House of Commons is a circular room 55 feet across. The *Four Courts*, or Courts of Law, near Richmond Bridge, built between 1776 and 1800, by Corley and Gandon, a noble range 450 feet by 170, with a fine portico, and a dome 64 feet span. The *Custom House*, near the Drogheda terminus, built in 1791, by Gandon, cost more than half a million, and being too large for the shipping business only, the Poor Law Board and other boards, are quartered here. River front 375 feet long, and dome 125 feet high, with a figure of Hope at the top. The *Post Office*, built in 1818, by Johnston, 223 feet long, with an Ionic portico. The *Inns of Court*, near the Midland Railway terminus, 110 feet long. The *Royal Exchange*, on Cork Hill near the Castle, built in 1779, by Corley, a beautiful Corinthian pile 100 feet square. The *National Educational Buildings* are at Old Tyrone House, with excellent training school attached, which the Queen has visited. *Kilmainham Hospital*, or Irish Chelsea Hospital, founded in 1680, and built by Wren, is on a small scale, with but 250 soldiers. An old brick pile, about 300 feet square, with part of preceptory of Knights Templars in the chapel. The Queen visited the old men in their dining hall, which has portraits. *Dublin Castle*, the Viceroy's seat since 1560, is in Dame Street, on Cork Hill, near College Green, and consists of two large courts, including government offices, St Patrick's beautiful hall, armoury, chapel royal (the Viceroy attends every Sunday morning), in the modern Gothic style, and the great Birmingham Tower, where the records are kept. This is the oldest part, dating as far back as 1411. There are portraits of Viceroys in the council chamber.

Dublin's trams

Above: Dublin & Blessington (No. 2) steam tram, a double-cabbed 2-4-2 built by T. Green & Son of Leeds & London. These operated between Terenure in Dublin and Blessington in County Wicklow, from 1888 until 1932. *(National Library of Ireland/wiki)*

Left: The shape of the city's modern trams, the Dublin Light Rail System, which entered service in 2004. It is known as the Luas, the Irish for 'speed'. *(David Jones)*

Bottom left: Ireland, even in Bradshaw's time, was a land of revolution, with independence a demand of the militant Irish. 1916 saw the Easter Rising, where Dublin revolted. Here, British soldiers guard the Great Northern Main Line in Dublin.

The *Viceregal Lodge* is in Pheonix Park, on the west side of Dublin, with the chief secretary's house near it, and the depot for the great Irish Ordnance Survey, which extends over more than 1,600 sheets. The park is 7 miles round, and contains barracks, Zoological Gardens, the Wellington Pillar, 205 feet high, and another to Lord Chesterfield, with a phoenix upon it, in allusion to the common name, but the proper name is *fionn uisge*, or fine water, after a spring which rises in it.

TRINITY COLLEGE, founded in 1591, by Queen Elizabeth, and rebuilt by Sir W. Chambers, is on College Green, with a Grecian front of 308 feet, and is composed of three quadrangles or squares – Parliament Square, 560 feet long, has the Chapel, Museum, etc. In Library Square is a fine room 210 feet long, with 150,000 volumes, the harp of Brian Boru, and Archbishop Usher's books, Wickliffe's MSS., and the *Book of Kells*, in which the Queen and Prince Albert have inscribed their names. The Provost's house is in Botany Bay Square. Portraits of Queen Elizabeth, Swift, Grattan, etc., are in the Theatre and Refectory; the gardens cover 20 acres. Usher, Berkeley, Swift, Goldsmith, Burke, O'Connell, Moore, etc., were of this college. The fellowships are not only well endowed, but the fellows are allowed to marry. Residence not being enforced, graduates come up only for examination.

CITY AND COUNTY BUILDINGS – The Mansion House, in Dawson Street, where the Lord Mayor lives; portraits of viceroys and sovereigns. The Sessions House, built in 1797; County Gaol at Kilmainham; Newgate Prison, built in 1773, by Cooley; Richmond Bridewell, for women. Commercial Buildings, in Dame Street, which contain Stock Exchange, Chamber of Commerce, etc. Corn Exchange, on Burgh Quay, the defunct Conciliation Hall. City Police Barracks for 1,150 men, near an old (Marsh's) gate; Old Linen Hall, now used as stores, contains 575 rooms, and covers 3 acres. Markets at Smithfield, Spitalfields, Boot Lane, etc. Cemeteries at Harold's Cross and Glasnevin, one 27 acres, the other 20 acres; at the latter Curran and O'Connell are buried.

SOCIETIES, HOSPITALS, etc. – Royal Dublin Society at old Leinster House, 140 feet long, founded in 1731. Excellent museums of minerals, agricultural implements, busts, etc., and a Botanical Garden at Glasnevin, near the Cemetery. The King's Inn Library, Royal Irish Academy in Dawson Street, near the College, with a museum of Irish antiquities; College of Surgeons on Stephen's Green, with a Doric front, large museum, etc. Blue Coat Hospital at Oxmantown; a front of 300 feet. Sir Patrick Dun's Hospital, founded in 1781. County Hospital, on the site of a garden formerly belonging to Dean Swift. Military Hospital. Dr Morse's Lying-in-Hospital, founded in 1745, near the Rotunda, in the Rutland Gardens, where public meetings are held. Claremont Deaf and Dumb and the Richmond Blind Schools. County Lunatic Asylum at Richmond. There are about 100 schools of all classes, attended by 16,000 children, and upwards of twenty benevolent societies.

PLACES OF AMUSEMENT, GARDENS, STATUES, etc. – The Theatre Royal is in Hawkins Street; the Queen's Royal, Great Brunswick Street; the Music

Above: The hustle and bustle of a busy Sackville Street, now known as O'Connell Street. The great Pillar, on which Admiral Nelson perched, was built in 1809 and felled in 1966 by a bomb planted by Irish Nationalists. Today the modern Spire of Dublin stands on the site. *(LoC) Below*: Footbridge at Churchdown, Dublin. *(National Library of Ireland/wiki)*

Hall, Lower Abbey Street. Portobello Gardens and the Phoenix Park Zoological Gardens. Archbishop Marsh's library contains 17,000 volumes; the Dublin Library is in D'Olier Street. The Statues are – Nelson, on a column 120 feet high, in Sackville Street; George II on St Stephen's Green, which is nearly a mile round (United Service Club and Archbishop Whateley's house here); William III, a bronze, on College Green, opposite Trinity College; George I in Dawson Street; George III (by Bacon) in the Peers' Room at the Bank, another, by Van Nost, stands in the Exchange; George IV in the Linen Hall; Sir M. O'Loghlen in the Four Courts. Merrion Square is the second in size.

BRIDGES – Nine in all, 100 to 250 feet long. Beginning at the east side are – Carlisle, on three arches; Wellington, of iron; Essex, on five arches, 250 feet long; Richmond, near the Four Courts; Whitworth, on the site of Ormonde Bridge, which was rebuilt in 1428; Queen's, built in 1768; Barrack, on four arches (the oldest); King's, of iron; Sarah, in one arch.

CHURCHES – Nearly sixty churches and chapels belong to the Establishment; a modern cathedral, nine churches, and eighteen convents, etc., to the Roman Catholics; and about twenty-five other chapels. There are two cathedrals in the dirtiest part of the city, both much altered. *Christ Church*, the oldest (marked by a tower), is a mixture of Norman and Gothic of the 12th century, in the shape of a cross, 230 feet long. One effigy is that of Strongbow, the first conqueror of Ireland, dated 1170. *St Patrick's* is an early English cross (with a spire), rebuilt in 1362, with buttresses, etc., and 300 feet long. It contains the Archbishop's throne, banners of the Knights of St Patrick, a bust of Dean Swift, monuments of Stella and Duke of Schomberg, and brasses (the only ones in Ireland) of the Wallops, etc. *St Andrew's* is a very fine modern Gothic church. *St George's*, by the same architect (Johnston), is a Grecian church, with a spire 200 feet high. *St Audeon's* is an old Gothic. *St Anne's*, a modern Gothic, has the grave of Mrs Hemans. *St Michan's* and *St Peter's* are large cross churches. Another *St Michan's*, belonging to the Roman Catholics, is a Gothic chapel. The Roman Catholic Archbishop's, or the *Conception Church*, is a large Doric edifice, built in 1816. *St Andrew's Chapel* is in the same style.

A list of the antiquities about Dublin may be seen in *Wakeman's Hand Book*. Round Towers are left at Clondalkin and Swords. Howth and Malahide Castles are on the Drogheda line. Up the Liffey are the Strawberry Beds, near Woodlands; Lucan and Leixlip Castles, near the Salmon Leap; Maynooth College; and Carton (a portion of which was destroyed by fire in 1855), the Duke of Leinster's seat.

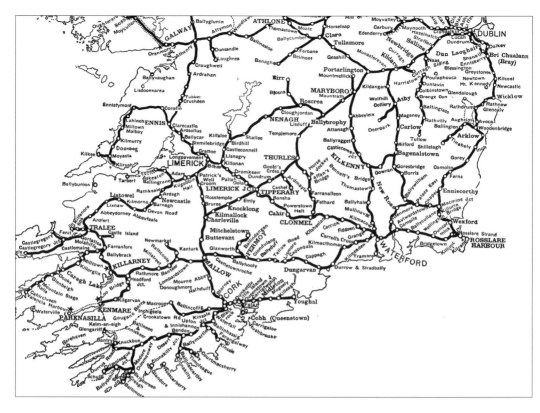

Above: Map of the Great Southern Railways showing the lines to the south and west of Dublin, published by the Viceregal Commission in 1906. Many of the smaller lines, and those at the extremities of the network, had not been built when Bradshaw's guidebook was first published in 1863. *Below*: Soldiers waiting for a train on the platform of Newbridge station, County Kildare, c. 1910. The Newbridge barracks was nearby, on the main street, but was closed after Independence. *(National Library of Ireland/wiki)*

GREAT SOUTHERN AND WESTERN

Dublin to Cork and Killarney

Leaving Dublin on this route we pass the station of CLONDALKIN to that of LUCAN, and enter immediately the county of

Kildare in the province of Leinster. Nearly one-fifth part of this county is occupied by bog, including a considerable portion of the great chain of morasses termed the Bog of Allen. In other parts the county has a surface slightly undulated, but in no instance does it assume a mountainous character. Pursuing our course via the stations of HAZLEHATCH, STRAFFON and SALLINS, we arrive at

NEWBRIDGE

A distance of 25½ miles from Dublin. A little to the left of the line is the *Curragh Race Course*, the 'Newmarket' of Ireland, on a fine down 6 miles long; also an encampment on a large scale, rendered memorable by the temporary sojourn of the Prince of Wales in the summer of 1861 to acquire a more thorough knowledge of military discipline.

The next station arrived at is Kildare, the junction of the lines to Carlow and Kilkenny.

KILDARE JUNCTION (Kildare)

Distance from station, 1 mile. A telegraph station.

MARKET DAY – Thursday.

FAIRS – February 12, April 5, May 12, June 29, and November 19.

RACES – Last week in April, 2nd Monday in June September, and October, on the Curragh.

The capital of a county of the same name, and cathedral town, near the Barrow, with a population of about 2,666. It belongs to the Fitzgeralds, represented by the Duke of Leinster. Formerly it was noted for the monastery of St Bridget, whose bright vestal lamp was kept constantly burning in her cell, of which there are some remains. She lived (as monkish writers say) contemporary with St Patrick, and is buried with him at St Columb, at Downpatrick. The cathedral, which is half a ruin, on the hill above the town, contains the Fitzgerald tombs. Close to it is a perfect *Round Tower*, 132 feet high. There are also remains of a castle, built by the English in the 14th century. The diocese is now incorporated with Dublin.

About 15 miles east are the Wicklow Mountains. To the north is the great Bog of Allen, part of the vast tract of bog which fills the centre of Ireland.

Great Bog of Allen, swallow down
That odious heap called Philipstown,

Old Huts, Curragh Camp

Above: The Curragh is Ireland's most famous racecourse, although Curragh was also the main British army barracks in Ireland. It is now the headquarters of the Irish army.

Below: Great Southern Railways No. 236, a class J22 0-6-0. This long-serving locomotive was built by Dubbs in 1895 and not scrapped until 1951.

And if thy maw can swallow more,
Pray take – and welcome! – Tullamore.

These two unhappy towns are planted in the very heart of this most desolate bog.

Kildare to Carlow, Kilkenny, & Waterford

Passing Athy, on the Barrow, where there is an old castle, built by Lord Kildare in 1506, and has Markets on Tuesday and Saturday, and Fairs March 17th, April 25th, June 9th, July 10th, October 11th, and December, we then proceed to *Mageny*, and enter

Carlow, a county in the province of Leinster, which returns two members, in the south-east part of Ireland. It is very fertile, both for tillage and pasture, and produces the best butter in the country. That portion which lies west of the River Barrow is mountainous, as is also that part which borders the county of Wicklow, but its general appearance is very picturesque and beautiful. It possesses inexhaustable quarries of limestone, beds of marls and different clays. In the mountains are found excellent iron ore, oxide of manganese, etc.

CARLOW
 A telegraph station.
 HOTEL – The Club House.
 MARKET DAYS – Mondays and Thursdays.
 FAIRS – May 4, June 22, August 26, and November 8.

CARLOW, the capital town of the county, with a population of about 9,940, who return one member, and are employed in the grain and butter trade, is built on the east bank of the River Barrow. The remains of a fine ruin overhang the river, and the ruins of St Keran's abbey, a convent, and a Catholic college, founded in 1795, and a Roman Catholic cathedral, with a monument to Bishop Doyle; a church with a spire of 195 feet high. In the vicinity, *Oak Park*, Colonel Bruen, and *Browne Hill*, W. Browne, Esq., are the principal objects of interest. The castle is supposed to have been built by King John, to secure the passage of the Barrow. It was taken by The Fitzgerald in 1495, 1534, and the rebels in 1641, and it continued a fortress for several centuries. Here black fetid rain fell in 1849, which the cattle refused to drink.

Passing MILFORD, we soon reach BAGENALSTOWN, close to which is the seat of J. Newtown, Esq., and then proceed to GOWRAN, where there are ruins of a castle built by the Ormondes, and burnt in 1650; and an early English church, with a font, and monuments of the Butlers: and Fairs are held March 8th, May 9th, August 10th, October 6th, and December 8th.

The branch to Wexford turns off here to the left and runs through Borris to

Left: Kilkenny Castle, one of the great houses of Ireland, was sold to the Irish government in 1967 for £50. It has subsequently been restored and is now one of Ireland's major tourist attractions.

Above: In stark contrast to the large houses of Ireland are the homes of the local populace. Even at the turn of the twentieth century, many lived in ramshackle hovels, such as these in Newtownbarry, Wexford, now renamed Bunclony, photographed by a tourist in August 1901.

BALLYWILLIAM, the extent of the present opening of the line in that direction. Leaving Bagenalstown, we now enter the county of

Kilkenny, the general aspect of which is hilly, but the elevations are seldom so precipitous or severe as to preclude the operations of the plough. The marble and coal of this county take rank as its most valuable productions. Mineral waters are found in several parts of the county; the most celebrated is termed the Spa of Ballyspellan, and situated in the parish of Farlagh. The banks of the Nore often present much pleasing scenery, particularly near the bridge of Ballylurch and the town of Ross. The lovely scenery on the banks of the Suir is truly worthy of the traveller's investigation. The county returns two members.

KILKENNY

A telegraph station. HOTEL – Callanan's.
MARKET DAYS – Wednesdays and Saturdays.
FAIRS – March 28, Corpus Christi, cattle and wool.

KILKENNY – This old capital of the 'Pale', or limit of English authority, was founded by Strongbow in 1172, and is now the chief town of Kilkenny county, a parliamentary borough, with one member, and seat of a diocese, on the River Nore, which is crossed by two bridges uniting it to Irishtown on the east side. Population about 4,100, who are engaged in the grain, provision, starch trade, etc. The Ormonde or Butler family have held possession of the town since 1400. Among the events which distinguish it, the principal one was the meeting of the Roman Catholic Supreme Council in 1642, after the great massacre in the preceding year, and during the distractions of the civil war in England. They met in an old building, now Huleatt's Commercial House.

Good stone and dark marble are abundant in this locality; most of the houses are of this material. One of the best views of the town is from John's bridge, another from Green's bridge. *Kilkenny Castle*, the seat of the Marquis of Ormonde, is finely seated on a rock above the river; it has been restored in the baronial style, and contains much old tapestry, as well as a gallery of the Butler portraits, by Lely and other artists of the 17th century, among which are portraits of Charles I and II, James II, and other Stuarts. Those of the great Duke of Ormonde and his gallant son should be noticed. Many of the family are buried in the cathedral, which is a small cross of the 13th century, 226 feet long, with a good east window and a fine prospect from the summit. Here are monuments of the Graces, who had a castle where the Court House now stands. St John's Church, once part of an abbey, also contains monuments of both families.

The Bishop's Palace, Chapter House, and a fine round tower, 108 feet high, are near the cathedral. At the college on the river, founded by the Butlers, Bishop Berkeley, Swift, and Congreve were educated. There is also a Roman Catholic College in the Gothic style, in Cork Road, called St Kyan's. One of their chapels is placed on the fine ruins of an abbey in Irishtown, founded in 1225,

Waterford

Left: A station kiosk at Waterford, *c.* 1924. Note the news placard, 'Wanted: One Honest Politician'. Some things never change. *(National Library of Ireland/wiki)*

Lower left: The bridge at Waterford. On the River Suir, Waterford was once a large port with over 200 ships registered there.

Below: The quays at Waterford. Throughout the medieval period, Waterford was Ireland's second city after Dublin. Ship building and glass making flourished here and it is still famed for its crystal glass. *(LoC)*

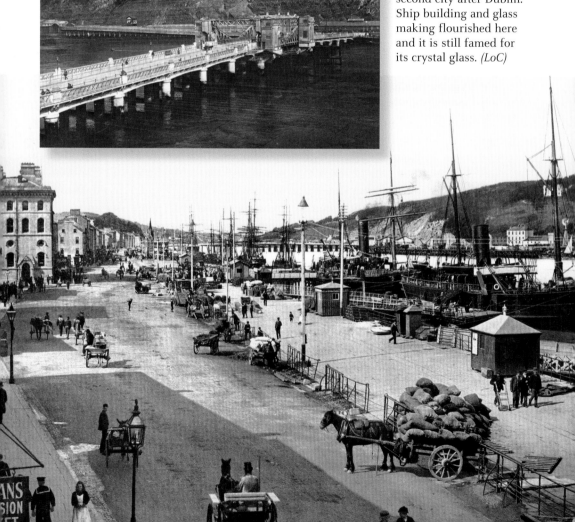

by the Pembrokes. Butler's grammar school, where Swift, Congreve, Farquhar, Harris, the antiquary, and Bishop Berkeley were educated. Here Clynn wrote his *Annals*. A pleasant promenade, called the Mall, is laid out on the Nore behind the town. Banim, the novelist, was a native.

The country becomes more hilly both up and down the Nore, towards its head, north and west of Kilkenny.

Dunmore Park and caves, belonging to the Ormondes; Tullaroan old church, near Courtown Castle, once the seat of the powerful Grace family, descended from Raymond le Gros. Ballyspellan Spa, near Johnstown, and the collieries in the Dysart Hills (the highest is 1,028 feet high), round Castle Corner. Here the Kilkenny or anthracite coal is quarried, in thin dirty seams; it burns without flame or smoke.

Passing BENNETT'S BRIDGE, where there are some large flour mills, and at which Fairs are held on February 24th, August 26th, September 19th, and December 21st, we proceed down the Nore, and come to THOMASTOWN and Innistroge Castle, with Mount Brandon, a granite peak 1,696 feet high, to the left, overlooking the Barrow; beyond which are Blackstairs and Leinster mountains, the latter on the Wexford borders, 2,600 feet high. Then passing BALLYHALE, we proceed to MULLINAVATT, where Fairs are held March 29th, September 2nd, October 3rd, and 28th, December 9th, and soon after reach KILMACOW, and then enter the county of

Waterford – This county is in the province of Munster, and returns two members. It is bounded on the north by the River Suir, on the west by the county of Cork, on the east by the harbour of Waterford, and on the south by the Atlantic Ocean. The eastern portion of the comity is low and fertile.

WATERFORD

A telegraph station.

HOTELS – Commin's, commercial and family, on the Quay; Dolbyn's, Commercial Buildings.

MARKET DAYS – Monday, Wednesday, Thursday, and Saturday.

FAIRS – May 4, June 24, October 4.

The capital of Waterford county, and a parliamentary borough, port, etc., in the south of Ireland. The River Suir, upon which it stands, divides the county from Tipperary, and joins the Barrow a few miles below, making the distance to the open sea about 14 miles. Population, about 29,300, who return two members, and are engaged chiefly in the provision trade. About 200 vessels, mostly of small tonnage, belong to the port; it has a thriving provision trade with Bristol, Liverpool, etc., and is provided with excellent quay-room, and water deep enough for ships of 1,000 tons.

The ancient Irish called it by several figurative names; but when the Danes settled here, in the 9th century, they styled it *Vater-fiord*, the 'Father harbour', on account of its superiority. Here they built a round tower, called the *Ring*, or

Left: No. 4, a small Manning Wardle & Co. 'H' class 0-4-0 saddle tank, in Waterford in 1905. *Below:* A steam-powered digger at work on the new railway cutting at Waterford. The terminus of the Waterford–Cork line was in Waterford South station in Bilberry until a new railway bridge was constructed across the Suir, allowing the move to the present station site in 1905. *(National Library of Ireland/wiki)*

Right: Reginald's Tower was built in 1003 as part of the city wall. It is the oldest civic building in Ireland, and the oldest to retain its Viking name. Located on the quayside, it currently houses the Waterford Viking Museum. *(LoC)*

Reginald's Tower, which, as it still exists, must be one of the oldest in Ireland, after the Round Towers. Another event was the marriage of Richard de Clare, or Strongbow, to the King of Leinster's daughter, Eva, which has been painted by Maclise. Here, too, Henry II landed, as 'Lord of Ireland', in 1172. Thenceforth it was steadfastly loyal to the English crown, as in Perkin Warbeck's attempt to take it, and during the civil war, when Cromwell was repulsed. Among the latest events was the embarkation of James II after the battle of the Boyne. It has returned two members to parliament almost ever since 1374.

The *Custom House* is a large building on the Quay. Further up the Suir, near Davis's brewery, is a curious *Wooden Bridge*, on thirty-nine arches, 832 feet long; it was built in 1794, by Cox, of Boston, in America, and leads over to the ship yards at Ferrybank, and a hill called Mount Misery. Two or three bridges cross John's River, a small stream which flows through the town, named after King John, who resided here when Governor of Ireland, in a palace, of which there are some remains in a crypt at the Deanery, in the Mall. Close to this wide thorough-fare is the *Cathedral of Waterford* diocese (now merged into Cashel); it is a modern building, of no particular character, with a steeple, and various effigies preserved from the former church. Among them is a curious figure of one Rice, with worms, etc., crawling over him, and designed, it is said, from his body as it appeared a year after his death. St Olave's Church is older than the present cathedral, though built only in 1734. There is a *Roman Catholic Cathedral*, and a College, with several professors attached.

The *Court House* was built by Gandon, the celebrated architect of some of the finest Dublin structures.

A large *House of Correction*, in Gaol Street, near Bally Bricker Green, where the gallows is set up. *Barracks* for the artillery in Morrison's Road. *Lunatic Asylum*, at John's Hill. The *County Hospital* is on the site of one founded by King John, and hand-somely endowed. There is another ancient endowment called Holy Ghost Hospital, now an asylum for widows; it was founded in the 13th century; its chapel is a ruin. There are various scientific, literary, and benevolent societies, among which are the *Christian Brothers' School*, and Bishop Gore's Hospital for ten clergymen's widows. The *Fever Hospital* was built in 1799, being the oldest for that object in Ireland. At present there is one in every county. *Fanning's Institution* for poor tradesmen, etc., was founded in 1843. Glass, starch, etc., are made here. In the vicinity are *Barron Court*, Sir H. W. Barron, Bart., M.P.; *New Park*, Rev. Sir J. Newport, Bart.; *Belmont*, R. Roberts, Esq.

Among the natives of Waterford were *Wadding*, the founder of the Irish Franciscan College at Rome, Archbishop Lombard, and Hartrey the historian. The Earl of Shrewsbury takes the title of Earl of Waterford from this town, which was granted to his ancestor in 1447; and it gives that of Marquis to the Beresford family.

Proceeding down the Suir, you come to Cheek Point, opposite *Dimbody Abbey* and the junction with the Barrow, and formerly a packet station for Bristol,

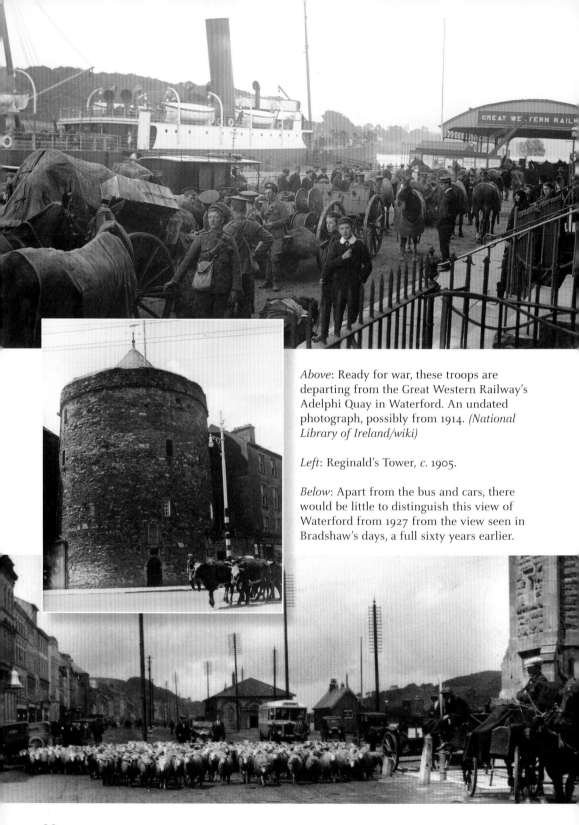

Above: Ready for war, these troops are departing from the Great Western Railway's Adelphi Quay in Waterford. An undated photograph, possibly from 1914. *(National Library of Ireland/wiki)*

Left: Reginald's Tower, *c.* 1905.

Below: Apart from the bus and cars, there would be little to distinguish this view of Waterford from 1927 from the view seen in Bradshaw's days, a full sixty years earlier.

etc. Passage is a part of Waterford borough, though 6 miles distant. There is a ferry to Dungannon on the Wexford side of the river, from which James II took his farewell of Ireland. *Dunmore*, at the mouth, is a bathing place, with a deserted pier harbour, which originally cost £100,000, and was made for the Milford Mail Packets. Some Druid stones are near. All the coast from this point, westward, past Tramore, is exposed and dangerous; but at Dungarvan which returns one member, and has two good hotels (Eagle, Mary Power, and Devonshire Arms, Mrs Magrath), there is a tolerable haven, with a ruined abbey, castle, etc. Opposite Dunmore is the *Hook Point* and *Light*, with an ancient tower, commanding a splendid view. It is a joke of the philologists, that when the conqueror of Ireland landed he said, 'he would take it by *Hook* or by *Crook*, and that the brave inhabitants of Fethard fought hard'; hence, say they, these names are derived. Fethard is near *Loftus*, the Marquis of Ely's seat (where they show Strongbow's sword), *Tintern Abbey* (a ruin), and *Bannow Bay*, which, like all the Wexford shore, is choked with sand hills.

There are an immense number of old forts built by the Norman invaders along this part of Ireland. Up the Suir, from Waterford, are, *Kilmeaden Castle*, which belongs to Lord Doneraile. Portlaw has a large cotton factory, established by the Malcomsons in 1818. *Curraghmore*, close to it, is the princely seat of the Marquis of Waterford; a large park and fine prospects. *Carrick-on-Suir,* a prosperous town, with a trade in corn, butter, etc., the land being rich and fertile. There is a Castle of the Butlers. Above this is *Clonmel*, where Sterne was born in 1713; and where the O'Brien *pronunciamento* was knocked on the head in 1848, the leader of which has returned to his native land, 'a wiser and better man', having been pardoned by Her Majesty Queen Victoria. To the south are the fine rugged mountains of the Cummeragh, a name synonymous with the Cumraeg, or Cimbri, by whose descendants they are still peopled. *Manorbullach*, the highest point, is 2,498 feet above the sea. Fine black and red trout are seen in the lakes. The Knockmealdown and Galtee mountains, some of which are 1,200 to 1,600 feet high, further west, are continuations of this range. Up the Barrow. This fine stream takes name from *burragh*, a bar boundary, as it was long the boundary of the English dominion, or 'Pale', in Ireland. New Ross was founded by Strongbow's daughter, Rose Macruine. It has a good trade in salmon and provisions. A wooden drawbridge crosses the river, which admits vessels of even 800 tons burden. Up the quay. It was the scene of much fighting in the rebellion of 1798, when Harvey and his followers were defeated by General Johnson. Here the first Temperance Society was established, in 1824. On the Wexford road is the Barn of *Scullabogue*, where 140 loyalists were burnt and shot by the rebels in 1798, under Father Murphy. Their General, Harvey, left on account of this massacre, but was captured in his hiding-place, on the Galtee Islands, and executed at Wexford, by sentence of court-martial.

Above: At Portarlington, Arthur Wellesley and his brother were educated. Arthur would go on to become the Duke of Wellington, who would defeat Napoleon, shown here, at the Battle of Waterloo in 1815.

Below: A general view of Athlone, at the head of the Athlone branch, in the 1920s.

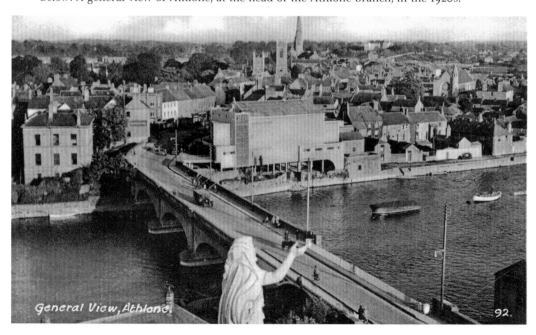

Kildare to Cork

We now return to Kildare, the point of deviation to Carlow, etc., and soon reach *Monastereran*, where are ruins of a monastery, built in the 7th century, rebuilt in the 8th, and refounded in the 12th, by the O'Dempseys. There is a Market here on Saturdays, and Fairs on March 28th, May 29th, July 31st, and December 8th. We now enter

King's County, which returns two members, and which, with the exception of Shevebloom Mountains, on its southern borders, is in general of a flat character, containing a great part of the ancient plain of Ireland. In 1801 nearly half the contents of the county were bog, mountain, and waste, or not arable land. Great part of the Bog of Allen lies within the county limits; several tracts have been reclaimed, but not to a great extent. The continuous bogs and levels preclude all possibility of picturesque beauty.

PORTARLINGTON

A telegraph station.
MARKET DAYS – Wednesday and Saturday.
FAIRS – January 5th, March 1st, Easter Monday May 22nd, July 4th, September 1st, October 12th and November 23rd.

PORTARLINGTON, returns one member, was formerly called Coltodry, and given by Charles II to Lord Arlington, who sold it to Sir P. Kout, who forfeited it. William III gave it to General Renvigny, who built the churches. In one of the schools at this place, the late 'Iron Duke' [the Duke of Wellington], and his brother, the Marquis of Wellesley, were educated.

ATHLONE BRANCH

GEASHILL. Here is O'Dempsey's Castle; Fairs are held on May 1st, October 6th, and December 26th.

TULLAMORE

A telegraph station.
MARKET DAYS – Tuesday and Saturday.
FAIRS – March 19, May 10, July 10, Sept. 13, Oct. 21, Dec. 13.

Here are the ruins of Sragh Castle, near those of Ballycowan. The population of the town is employed in the linen trade.

Great Southern and Western Main Line continued

Queen's County returns two members, in the eastern division of which the range of the Dysart Hills forms a prominent and picturesque object, rising

Advertising poster for the Great Southern Railways featuring a highly romanticised view of the locals. Although why Ireland is portrayed as a 'Land of Eternal Youth' is unclear. Fortunately Bradshaw's observations are more down to earth.

in a detached group from the flat country by which they are surrounded. These hills command the view of a rich and beautiful country, adorned with extensive plantations and splendid demesnes. Considerable quantities of corn are produced in this county, and large tracts of land are profitably appropriated to pasturage.

MARYBOROUGH

A telegraph station. This place has a population of 3,673, engaged in the flax trade, and contains remains of an old castle, founded in 1560, ruins of an old church, and raths. Markets are held here on Thursdays; and Fairs January 1st, February 24th, March 25th, May 12th, July 5th, September 4th, October 26th, and December 12th.

We then proceed to MOUNTRATH, where Markets are held on Saturdays, and Fairs, February 17th, May 8th, June 20th, August 10th, September 19th, and November 6th.

Tipperary, a county in the province of Munster, which returns two members, and consists of twelve baronies. It contains some of the most productive districts in the country; the peasantry, however, are the most riotous, distressed, and poverty-stricken. Trade and manufactures are scarcely known out of the large towns. Water-power might be produced to any extent in this part of Ireland, and it is only necessary for the hand of industry to be rightly directed to ensure the most abundant return.

ROSCREA

A telegraph station.

Contains a population of about 9,690, engaged in the coarse woollen factories, and has ruins of a castle built by King John in 1213. In the churchyard are the porch, etc., of an old abbey, St Cronan's spire, and a round tower 80 feet high. A Roman Catholic Cathedral, with a tower of the Franciscan Friary, founded in 1490, and large infantry barracks (formerly the Damers' seat). Markets are held here on Thursday and Saturday, and Fairs on March 25th, May 27th, June 21st, August 8th, October 9th, and November 29th. Near at hand are *Borristown*, and *Corville*, the seat of the Hon. W. F. Pritie, and pass on to

TEMPLEMORE, which is situated on the River Suir, under the Devil Bit Mountains, and contains large infantry barracks, capable of holding 1,500 men. Close at hand are the *Priory*, the seat of the Cardens, ruins of the Knights Templars' Castle, and *Lloydsborough*, J. Lloyd, Esq., and we soon after reach

THURLES

A telegraph station.
HOTEL – O'Shee's.
MARKET DAYS – Tuesday and Saturday.
FAIRS – 1st Tuesday in the month, Easter Monday, Aug. 21, and Dec.

Above: Locomotive No. 74 at the Cashel (Cahir) railway station, at the foot of the Rock of Cashel, south Tipperary. The Cashel Extension Railway arrived in October 1904 and to save money the buildings were of a very simple corrugated-iron construction. *(National Library of Ireland/wiki)*

Above: The Siege of Limerick during the 1690 rebellion.

Here the Danes and English were defeated in the 10th century, by O'Brien, who built the Castle. Carmelite Monastery, and Knights Templar's preceptory. It contains a population of about 10,300, chiefly engaged in the corn trade. Close at hand are the ruins of a monastery, and two castles. Then, passing Goold's Cross, 4½ miles from which is *Cashel*, the ancient seat of the Kings of Munster, whose palace stood on the Rock of Cashel, as also did a church built by St Patrick, whose effigy is here, on the site of which are the ruins of Cormac's chapel, 53 feet long, built in 1134, by Cormac Macarthy, having frescoes, which being discovered by Archdeacon Cotton, he restored the pile. The old early English Cathedral, built by King Donald O'Brien, in 1169, 210 feet by 170, has a monument to Archbishop Macgragh, and was used until 1745; Archbishop Median's Vicars Choral Hall, built in 1421. The Episcopal Palace, Archbishop M'Gruvill's Cistercian Abbey, built in 1260, with the tribute stone, and round tower of freestone, 90 feet high, and 56 in girth. Bore Abbey, founded by that Archbishop in 1272, lies to the west, and in the town there is an old friary. Here Henry II was confirmed monarch of Ireland, by Pope Alexander, in 1172. The Earl of Kildare burnt the cathedral, because he thought the Archbishop was in it, and in 1147, Lord Inchiquin captured it for the Parliament. Markets are held on Wednesday and Saturday, and Fairs on the 26th March, 7th August, and 3rd Tuesday in every month. We continue the route to Dundrum, close to which lies *Dundrum House*, the noble seat of the Viscount Hawarden.

Limerick, the surface of which, although in many places diversified by hills, is not, generally speaking, mountainous, excepting on the south-east, where it is bounded by the Galtees, a ridge of lofty mountains which extend into Tipperary and the borders of Kerry, where the ground gradually rises, and forms a grand amphitheatre of steep mountains, in a wide area from Loghill to Drumcolloher. Returns two members to parliament.

LIMERICK JUNCTION

At LIMERICK JUNCTION the line branches off to the right to

LIMERICK

A telegraph station.
HOTELS – Moore's, J. W. Moore, Clare, Catherine O'Brien; Cruise's Royal, Edward Cruise.
MARKET DAYS – Wednesday and Saturday.
FAIRS – Easter Tuesday, July 4, August 4, and Dec. 4.

This old seat of the O'Briens, now the capital of Limerick county, a parliamentary borough and a thriving port, has a population of about 67,000, who return two members, lies in a flat part of Munster, 50 miles from the mouth of the Shannon. Limerick is divided into Old Town and New Town. The latter, founded not more than eighty years ago, lies to the east, has some good streets and squares about Richmond Place and other quarters; while the Old (or Irish) Town, on King's

Limerick

Above: The station on Parnell Street was built by the Waterford & Limerick Railway and opened in August 1858. The station was renamed as Limerick Colbert in 1966. *(National Library of Ireland/wiki)*

Left: A view from around 1903 of children gathered for the photographer in front of the Treaty Stone at Limerick.

Island to the north, is one mass of dilapidation and filth; the old crumbling houses being used by the poor wherever they can find something like a roof to cover them. King's Island, which lies between the Shannon and a loop of it called Salmon Weir River, is joined to the opposite shore by Thomond Bridge, rebuilt in 1839, and to the New Town by New and Ball's (or Baal's) Bridges. The Wellesley Bridge, opposite New Town, is a handsome level stone way, on five arches, with a swing in the middle for shipping to pass into the floating docks. By a weir below this bridge, and new embankments, sufficient water is obtained to bring vessels of 600 tons alongside the quay. The Irish Western Yacht Club make Limerick their headquarters. About 15,000 tons of shipping belong to the port; the customs are nearly a quarter of a million. Vast quantities of beef, pork, bacon, butter for which it is particularly celebrated, and other 'Irish provisions', are exported. The provision stores of Messrs. Russell should be visited; they cover 3 acres, and here 50,000 pigs and 2,000 head of cattle are salted annually. One feature of it is a 'rat barrack' (or hole) where the rats are fed and periodically destroyed, and thus prevented from going to the stores. *Hall's Ireland.*

Excellent lace is made here by two or three firms; it is also noted for its fish-hooks, 'every hook worth a salmon', made by O'Shaughnessey; and delicate gloves, sold at Bourke's, but the best 'Limerick gloves' are now made at Cork.

The Cathedral of St Mary is an ill-shaped common looking Gothic building, begun by the O'Briens of Thomond on the site of their palace, having a square tower of 120 feet high, which affords a beautiful view. Thomond means North Munster, of which the O'Briens were kings. The unfortunate, misguided, but highly respected Mr O'Brien, whose attempted insurrection in 1848 ended so lamentably for himself, is their descendant. An older building is King John's Castle, at one end of Thomond Bridge, of which two heavy round stones and a gate are left. It was taken by Ireton (but through treachery) after a siege of six months, in 1641; and here he died of the plague the same year. At the other end of the Thomond Bridge (on the Clare side) is the famous Treaty Stone, shaped something like an arm-chair, upon which, it is stated, the treaty was signed on the 3rd of October, 1601, when James II's garrison of Irish and French surrendered to De Ginkell. One article stipulated that Roman Catholics should take the oath of allegiance, and should be preserved from any disturbance on account of their religion. This provision was adhered to by William III, but broken by Queen Anne: and hence the city of Limerick is called the 'City of the Violated Treaty'. Thus terminated the War of the Revolution in Ireland.

On the Roxborough road, near the *County Court* and *Gaol* (marked by a tower), is the large district Lunatic Asylum, 430 feet long. The *City Hall* was built in 1763. The *Chamber of Commerce* is at the Commercial Buildings.

Lord Chancellor Clare (Fitzgibbon) Speaker Pery, of the Irish Parliament, whose family are Earls of Limerick, and founders of the New Town, Archbishop Creagh, S. O'Halloran, W. Palmer, and Callopy, painters, were natives.

The scenery down the Shannon is not very tempting, but the rich correasses

Mayo-Composite Aircraft Separating over Rochester.

Above: Foynes would become in the 1930s a major seaplane base, with these majestic flying boats using the area to fly to Canada, the closest landfall. Mail was all-important and to get the range to fly to New York, the Mercury-Mayo composite aircraft was designed. The larger flying boat would take off with the mail plane attached and once a few hundred miles out would detach and the mail plane would fly on. Only one was ever built.

Below: Stereoscopic card showing O'Rourke's Tower, Clonmacnoise, which was named after the Connacht king, Fergal O'Rourke. The tower was finished in 1124 and, in 1135, it was struck by lightning. Next to it is a wonderfully carved Celtic cross. See page 114.

(85)-427-O'Rourke's Tower and great Cross, (N. W.) in sacred Clonmacnoise, Ireland.   Copyright   by Underwood & Underwood.

yield heavy crops of wheat and potatoes. At its mouth, on the south side, below Tarbert, is Ballybunian, a pretty watering place, noted for its caves. Kilrush, on the opposite shore, is a place which suffered dreadfully in the late famine, in common with all this quarter of Ireland; in which whole villages were depopulated. From its mouth to its source under Quilca Mountain in Cavan, Shannon is 250 to 260 miles long; a steamer runs up as far as Athlone. Some of the best parts are – the Falls, near Castle Connell; O'Brien's Bridge; the hills about Lough Derg, which has a round tower on Holy Island; Clonmacnois, above Shannon Bridge; and the mountain scenery of Lough Allen. Clonmacnoise, or Seven Churches, in particular, deserves notice as one of the seats of letters and religion in Ancient Irish times (i.e., before the Romish supremacy was known); there are ruins of a cathedral, two round towers, a palace, etc., and many graves.

In the middle of County Clare is Mount Callan, a fine peak 1,280 feet high, having a 'cromlech' (or sun altar), and an 'ogham stone' near the top. The cliffs on the coast to the west are wonderfully bold; those about Malbay and Moher drop sheer down to the sea for 600 to 1,000 feet. Here one of the Spanish Armada came ashore – at Spanish Point.

Limerick and Foynes

The line beyond Limerick turns westward, to

PATRICK'S WELL
The junction of the Cork and Limerick Direct, a line which very mush shortens the distance between Limerick and Cork. The railway passes the stations of CROOME and BRUREE to CHARLEVILLE, in connection with the Great Southern & Western Railway.

In the neighbonrhood of Patrick's Well are ADARE, at which are remains of an Austin Friary, O'Donovan's Castle, dismantled by Cromwell, and the Franciscan Abbey, and Adare Abbey, the beautiful seat of the Earl of Dunraven, the descendant of 'Con of the Hundred Battles', who, like the late peer, is one of the best landlords in Ireland, lives on his estates, and attends to the amelioration of his tenants. A number of German Protestants, called Palatines, have been settled here for a century. Markets are held here on Saturdays, and Fairs monthly, except in June, July, and August.

RATHKEALE – This place contains three castles of the Desmonds. Here also some of the Germans from the Palatinate are settled.

ASKEATON – Here is another of the Desmonds' castles, with a priory founded by them, and a church which was built by the Knights Templar.

Cork Kent station

Above: Photographed in around 1893, the year in which the station was opened by the GS&WR under its original name, Glanmire Road. The dark strips above the tracks are shields to protect the glass roof from the blast of the chimney stacks as the locos pull away. *(National Library of Ireland/wiki)*

Left: No. 36, a 3-foot gauge 2-2-2 built for the Great Southern Railways in 1848 that remained in service until 1874. With 6-foot driving wheels it was exhibited at the Cork Exhibition of 1902 and at the Stockton & Darlington centenary celebrations in 1925. Since 2007 it has been displayed on the concourse at Cork. *(Andrew Abbott)*

FOYNES

From this place steamers sail down the Shannon to Tarbert and Kalrush, from the former of which a very agreeable tour, via Tralee, may be made to Killarney. Maviston Abbey is near.

From Limerick the tourist may, if he be disposed, proceed onward by rail to Clare Castle, where are also the remains of a monastery built in 1290; also by another route to Castle Connel, at the southern extremity of Lough Derg, and Killaloe, with its cathedral and old churches. In the vicinity of this latter place, is *Kincora*, the ancient seat of Bian Boru, and the slate quarries in the Adra Hills; the Keeper and Doon Mountains, 2,265 feet high in one part; Lough Garnear Bruff surrounded by a remarkable quantity of Druid stones and a castle of the Desmonds, the last of whom is said to be buried under the lake.

Great Southern and Western Main Line continued

From Limerick Junction the line again turns off to the left for Clonmel and Waterford, a description of which latter town will be found on page 27.

Passing KNOCKLONG, which contains ruins of the O'Hurleys; the Lowes' and Clangibbons' Castles, and where fairs are held, May 23, and October 1, we proceed to

KILMALLOCK

FAIRS are held here on Feb. 21, March 25, June 9, July 6, Nov. 8, and Dec. 4, close at hand are *Mount Coote*, C. Coote, Esq.; *Ush Hill Tower*, E Evans, Esq.

Here are the ruins of a Dominican Friary, founded in 1291, and dismantled by Cromwell. The church, partly in ruins, contains a bell tower, and tombs of the Fitzgeralds. The fortified town walls and gates, with the stone-built houses, etc., etc., all exist as in old times, though in ruins; some dismantled by Cromwell.

CHARLEVILLE, close to which is Charleville Castle, the seat of the Earl of Charleville. We now enter the county of

CORK

Which greatly exceeds the other counties, both in population and extent, and returns two members. It reaches along the south coast of the island from Youghal Bay to the more westerly point of Beerhaven, a distance of 160 miles, and is remarkably mountainous. With the exception of a few spots of small extent, there is absolutely no level land; even the valleys, as they are called, are full of swells and ridges. The general appearance of the country is varied and beautiful, the principal defect being want of trees, which are seldom planted except by the great landowners. The richest part of this county is towards the north, and a great quantity of limestone is found in the fertile districts. The south coast has many excellent harbours, and abounds in rivers.

Blarney Castle

'Blarney Castle, built by M'Carthy in 1446, and visiting, if time will admit, the Blarney Stone, which has the founder's name upon it, and to kiss which the traveller must be lowered 20 feet, so that...'

Above: Colourised view of the castle tower, *c*. 1895.

Left: The castle featured on 'Land of Romance', a Great Southern Railways poster.

BUTTEVANT

called by Spenser 'gentle Mulla', where there are remains of a priory founded in 1290 by the Barrys, Earls of Barrymore, whose battle words were *Benter en avant*, Forward. Fairs are held here on March 27th, July 20th, October 14th, and November 22nd. Close at hand are *Buttevant Castle*, Sir J. C. Anderson, Bart., the ruins of the abbey, in which are the graves of those who fell in 1647 at Knockninoss, where Sir A. M'Donnell (William Colkille) was killed, and the remains of two old castles. To the east is *Kilcoleman Castle*, called by Spenser Kilnemullugh, and where he wrote his *Fairie Queen*.

MALLOW (Junction)

A telegraph station.

HOTEL – Imperial.

MARKET DAYS – Tuesday and Friday.

FAIRS – Feb. 10th, Monday before Shrove Tuesday, May 3rd and 12th, July 7th and 26th, Oct. 29th and 30th.

RACES in September.

BOATS 1s 6d per mile.

This place contains a population of about 9,975, who return one member, and are engaged in the tan and salt works. The church, built in 1818, close to the ruins of the old edifice, which contains some old tombs. Here are warm springs, similar to those at Clifton in Somersetshire, first used in 1740, by consumptive patients. Close to Aurabella is a viaduct of 515 feet, on ten arches, and the seat of R. Purcell, Esq., *Dromore*, A. Newman, Esq.; Murphy, the mathematician, was a native. Thence passing Blarney, where Fairs are held September 18th and November 11th, and Blarney Castle, built by M'Carthy in 1446, and visiting, if time will permit, the Blarney Stone, which has the founder's name upon it, and to kiss which the traveller must be lowered 20 feet, so that, according to the village rhymers, 'when having kissed it, nobody can refuse you anything'; and as a satire on which Millikan wrote the song, 'The Groves of Blarney, they are so charming'. A most beautiful prospect of the adjacent country can be obtained from the Stone.

CORK

A telegraph station.

HOTELS – Imperial, Royal, Victoria, Hibernian, George Street.

CARRIAGES and Carts at the station and hotels. For returning the same road as driven – if not kept waiting beyond half-an-hour – half the above rates; if detained beyond the half-hour, 1s to be paid for a one-horse covered carriage; for a jaunting car, 6d for each hour detained, and half fare back. If it is intended to hire the vehicle by time, intimation of such must be given to the driver prior to the engagement. After 12 at night the fares are doubled.

PADDY

PURE POT STILL WHISKY
TEN YEARS OLD
DISTILLED, MATURED, and BOTTLED BY
CORK DISTILLERIES CO., LTD.
CORK.

Left: Advertisement for Paddy Pure Pot Still Whisky, produced by the Cork Distilleries Co. Ltd. The blended whiskey was first produced in 1877 and is still distilled and bottled in Cork by Irish Distilleries.

Bradshaw makes several references to a 'car'. This has nothing to do with automobiles, but refers to the Jaunting or 'Outside' Car. These light two-wheelers carried tourists facing outwards to explore the attractions. An alternative was the 'Inside' car where, as the name suggest, they faced inwards. There was also a covered version. *Below*: A card for the tourist maket, depicting an Outside Car, flanked by illustrations of two Irish peasants. *(LoC)*

IRISH PEASANT
THE·IRISH JAUNTING OR "OUTSIDE CAR"
IRISH PEASANT GIRL.

Tariff of Jaunting Cars: Four-wheel carriage, 1s 3d per mile; two-wheel, 9d per mile. To Blackrock Castle, 1s 9d to 2s 3d; to Blarney, 2s 9d to 3s 3d; to Glanmire, 2s 3d to 3s 3d; to Queenstown, 5s 9d to 7s 3d; to Passage, 2s 9d to 4s 3d; to Queen's College, 1s to 1s 6d, driver included. Tariff doubled after 12 at night.

MARKET Days – Monday and Thursday, for cattle.

FAIRS – Trinity Monday and October 1st.

BANKERS – Provincial Bank of Ireland; Branch of Bank of Ireland; Branch of National Bank of Ireland.

A city, port, and capital of county Cork, and Munster province, on the River Lee. The rail reaches the town by a tunnel half a mile long. It has a population of about 86,485, engaged in the glass, cutlery, and glove manufactories, and returns two members. Its splendid naval harbour is 11 miles lower down. Cork is not older than the year 600, when an abbey was founded on a low island in the Lee, where most of the city now stands. From the surrounding marshes it derives its name (*Coreagh*). A long street or walk, called the Mardyke, crosses the island, which is united to both banks of the stream by nine bridges, the best of which is the Anglesea iron bridge. The suburbs to the north and south stand higher; on the south bank is the new City Park of 240 acres, near the Bandon Railway. As might be expected, it suffers when the floods come down. The houses are built of stone, either thatched or slated, with many narrow, dirty streets, and but few remarkable public buildings. *St Finbarr's Cathedral* is modern except the tower which belonged to the old one. On the site of Gill Abbey is the new *Queen's College*, a handsome quadrangular Gothic pile, by Sir T. Deane, opened in 1849, when the Queen visited the town; her statue is here. There was a castle where the Court House stands. A large *Lunatic Asylum*, for the county, on Shannock Hill. The Botanic Garden is now a public *Cemetery*, established by Father Mathew, the Capuchin friar, who began his first temperance society here, in 1838. Besides savings banks and loan funds, there is a *Mont de Pieté*, a pawnshop conducted on an economical principle for the benefit of the poor, imitated from those on the continent. There are large barracks on the hill above the town. A Museum at the Cork Institute, founded in 1807, and a good proportion of benevolent institutions for both creeds.

Cork is not a large seat of manufactures; a little glass, with some good cutlery and beer, are the chief products. Also Limerick gloves, so delicate as to be sold packed in a walnut shell. But there is a large export trade (to the value of £3,000,000) in grain, cattle, whisky, provisions, and especially country butter. About 400,000 firkins of the last went to market in 1850; it is duly classified and branded by a committee, and the prices fixed beforehand every market day.

Maclise and Barry the painters, Sheridan Knowles the dramatist, Dr Maginn, one of the first editors of *Fraser's Magazine*, the Right Hon. J. W. Croker, of the Quarterly, Murphy, the Spanish traveller, General O'Leary, Miss Thomson (the

Above: Patrick Street in Cork, with the newly opened tramway system in full operation. Trams came to Cork in 1898 and the system closed down in 1931.

Below: At Queenstown, now Cobh, there was a major port for emigrants heading from Ireland to Canada and the USA. Perhaps the two most famous ships to call here were the ill-fated *Titanic* and *Lusitania*. Large ships would anchor offshore and passengers were carried by tenders to the waiting vessel. It was here that *Titanic* made her last landfall before being sunk. Many of the emigrating Irish would have left from the White Star pier shown here.

Emperor Muly Mahomet's wife), Wood the antiquary, Milliken, Hogan, and Hastie, the Madagascar traveller, were natives.

The Lee, above Cork, may be ascended past Inniscarra and Macroom Castle, to the solitary lakes of Allua and Gongane Barra, and the Shahy Mountains, which are 1,796 feet high; thence over Priest Leap Pass to Glengariff, a distance of about 50 miles.

The river is lined with granite quays, (inaccessible at low water), at which large vessels can unload; but the general place for unloading is at Passage, lower down, to which there is a railway of eight miles; but the descent should be made by boat to enjoy the beautiful views of the hills and country seats on both sides, and Blackrock and Monkstown Castles. The noble harbour, surrounded by hills on all sides, is five miles long, inclusive of the islands in it, having room and water enough for hundreds of vessels of any size. In war time 400 sail have left under convoy in one day. From this port Raleigh started on his last voyage (1617) to Guiana; and the *Sirius*, Captain Roberts, the second steamer to cross the Atlantic, left on the 1st June, 1838, reaching New York in seventeen days. Queenstown (formerly Cove), is situated on a steep terrace, on Great Island, with its yacht club and pretty bathing rooms. It is a soft, sheltered spot for invalids. Here Wolfe, the author of 'Not a drum was heard', died of consumption. There is a convict depot on Spike Island; and an ordnance depot at Haulbowline Island. Forts and old castles are perched on the highest points of ground. From the sea the appearance of the entrance, at first, is rather gloomy and disappointing.

All the scenery of this fine county is of a striking character, whether inland or along the coast. Cloyne (15 miles) with its Cathedral, Round Tower, and Druid Stone; Castlemartyr Castle, near Lord Shannon's seat; Youghal (28 miles), on the coast, where is shown Raleigh's house and his myrtles, and the fine remains of a Collegiate Church; Mourne Abbey (13 miles), under the Nagle Mountains.

CORK AND BANDON

By the (single line) rail to Bandon, the coast about Clonakilty, Skibbereen, Cape Clear, and Bantry Bay, may be visited; and thence Glengariff and Hungry Hill, with their magnificent scenery. At the last is one of the most remarkable waterfalls in the kingdom, rivalling the Staubbach, in Switzerland. Cars may be hired, but a pedestrian trip is the true way to enjoy and make oneself acquainted with the country. The constant drizzle is the chief drawback, but this gives Ireland its emerald green. It is said there that it never leaves off but on the 30th of February.

The line passes WATERFALL, BALLINHASSIG, to the JUNCTION Station, at which point the branch of the railway, 10¾ miles long, runs to the left, via FARRANGALWAY, to...

The Lakes of Killarney
Bradshaw writes, 'The traveller who wishes to see the lakes, and be as near to them as possible, should not stay at the village, but take up his residence at one of the hotels near the Lake, not for the sake of avoiding the town, but for the convenience of being near the lakes and within full view of the magnificent mountain scenery.'

Left: 'Killarney – Heaven's Reflex.' A poster for the Great Southern Railways.

Below: A colour advertising postcard of the Royal Victoria Hotel's Autobus in County Kerry. 'Linking Railway and the Killarney Lakes – 4 minute run.'

with a population of about 6,970, who return one member. It contains a church (in which no townspeople will be married), with tombs of the Southwells, the ruins of Castle-in-Park, founded in 1334. Fairs are held here on May 4th, September 4th and November 21st, and Markets on Saturday and Wednesday. This place gives title to the De Courcys of Kinsale House, who are privileged to remain covered in the presence of the reigning sovereign. It was taken by the Spaniards in 1380, but recaptured from them in 1601. Sir E. Scott, in 1689, defended it for James II, who landed from Brest in the same year. Close at hand is *Ruthmore*, the seat of M. Cramer, Esq.

UPTON and BRINNY, in the vicinity of which are *Brinny House*, J. Nash, Esq.; *Upton*, the Rev. S. Payne.

INNOSHANNON ROAD, close to which are the ruins of Downdaniel and Shippool Castles. Here Fairs are held on May 29th and October 3rd; and in the vicinity are *Innoshannon Road*, seat of S. Adderley, Esq., and *Firgrove*, R. Quin, Esq., and then quickly proceed to

BANDON

Telegraph station at Cork, 20 miles.

HOTEL – French's.

MARKET DAY – Saturday.

FAIRS – May 6th and 25th, Holy Thursday, October 29th, November 8th, first Wednesday in every month, except May and November.

This place has a population of about 9,303, employed in the camlet stuff, linens, leather, flour, beer, and whisky trades, who return one member, and contains a grammar school, founded by the great Earl of Cork. It is celebrated for its salmon fisheries. Sir R. Cox and Dr. Brady, the psalmist, were natives.

Excursion to the Lakes Of Killarney

Scotland, Wales, and the most beautiful districts of England, whatever may be their attractions, do not offer much novelty to the majority of men who, in the excursion period of the year, rush from smoky London and the cares of business to feast their eyes upon the beauty, and allow their lungs to inhale the fresh air, of the fields, lakes, and mountains. To such persons we recommend a trip to Ireland, and the lovely Lakes of Killarney. The journey has been rendered comparatively moderate in cost, and convenient as regards time, by the arrangements of the London & North Western Railway Company. The directors issue excursion tickets for the entire journey there and back, giving the tourist fourteen days for the trip, and make all necessary arrangements with the Irish South Western Railway Company for passing him on to his destination.

From Dublin to Killarney is a distance of 186 miles. From a railway train the traveller can, in general, get only partial and unsatisfactory glimpses of the

Above: The terminus at Killarney opened in 1853, and to encourage tourism the GS&WR opened a hotel on the site. This was the first railway-owned hotel in Ireland. *(National Library of Ireland/wiki)*

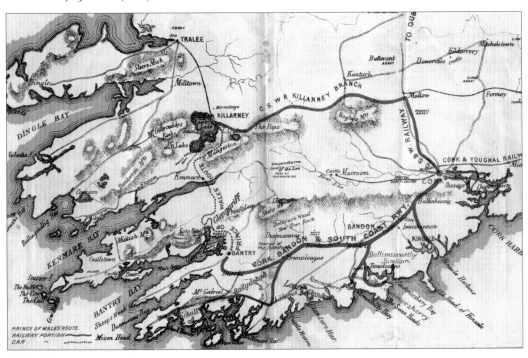

A map, from an 1892 guide to Killarney, of the Prince of Wales route to the Lakes of Killarney via Bantry, Glengariff and Kenmare, leaving Cork (Albert Quay Station) every morning at 9.20 and every evening at 3 o'clock.

country on either side of him; but such views as are obtained will impress the tourist on this route with the beauty of the scenery and the fertility of the soil. The course of the railway is through the counties of Dublin, Kildare, Queen's County, the 'nether tip' of King's County, Tipperary, Limerick, Cork, and Kerry.

From MALLOW JUNCTION the line proceeds to LOMBARDSTOWN, thence to KANTURK, which has an old castle belonging to the M'Carthys erected on the River Blackwater, 120 feet by 80. Fairs are held here on March 17th, May 4th, July 4th, September 29th, November 31st, and December 11th, and Markets on Saturdays, (Yelverton, Lord Avonmore, was a native).

MILL STREET. Markets are held here on Thursdays, and Fairs on January 6th, March 1st and 12th, June 1st, September 1st, and December 26th.

SHINNAGH and HEADFORD stations.

KILLARNEY

A telegraph station.

HOTELS – Finn's Royal Victoria Lake Hotel; Railway; Lake; Tore View; Keumare Arms; Royal Hibernian.

TARIFF OF CARS – Viz., one horse car, for two persons, 10d per mile; for three or four, 1s per mile. Carriage and pair horses, 1s 6d per mile. Ponies, 5s per day.

Two-oared boat, 7s 6d per day; four-oared, 15s; and six-oared, 21s per day. Car Drivers and Boatmen's hire included in the above charges. Guides are 3s 6d per day each, and Buglers, 5s.

BOATS on the lakes, 1s 6d per hour.

MARKET DAY – Saturday.

FAIRS – July 6th, August 10th, October 7th and 11th, November 28th, and December 28th.

BANKERS – National Provincial Bank of Ireland.

The traveller who wishes to see the lakes, and be as near to them as possible, should not stay at the village, but take up his residence at one of the hotels near the Lake, not for the sake of avoiding the town, but for the convenience of being near the lakes, and within full view of the magnificent mountain scenery. For boating or car riding the situation is equally convenient, and as starting places for all the celebrated spots, whether of islands or mountains, must be considered as far superior to any station in the interior of the town. On looking from the windows of these hotels, the traveller will see at a glance that the beauty of the Killarney Lakes and Mountains has not been exaggerated.

The ROYAL VICTORIA HOTEL, Thomas Finn, proprietor, situated near the lakes, is only a mile from the terminus of the Killarney Junction Railway, and also commands magnificent views. The lake shines like molten gold in the light of a morning sun; its numerous green and romantic islands stud its breast with beauty, and the mountains rear their majestic crests across the waters, hemming them in with sublimity. Among the most conspicuous is Mangerton

Above: A typical Irish peasant's cottage, usually with walls of mud or rough stone with a thatch of oat straw. Fires would be lit inside and the smoke escape through a hole in the roof. 'There is nothing in Ireland that strikes the eye of a non-native traveller, so much as the misery – the squalid misery of the habitation of our people. The tottering, crumbling, mud walls – the ragged, furrowed, and half rotten thatch – the miserable basket-shaped orifice that answers as a chimney – the window, with its broken panes stuffed with a wisp of straw, or some rags, filthy and nasty.' *Dublin Penny Journal*, 1833.

Below: While some hotels used buses from an early age, the 1950s saw the Arbutus Hotel still using gigs for their tours of the Lakes, starting from Killarney.

ARBUTUS HOTEL, KILLARNEY

SIGHTSEERS COMMENCING AN ARBUTUS TOUR

– the most round and lumpish of them all – celebrated for a lake about half way to its summit, called the Devil's Punch Bowl, the ascent to which is strongly recommended to all travellers. The Turk or Tore Mountain, the Purple Mountain, with its separate hills of Tomies and Glena; and the jagged, highly picturesque, and splendid range known as Mac Gillycuddy's Reeks bound the view, and impress the visitor with a deep sense of their grandeur and beauty. We do not assert that the lake scenery of England and Scotland is inferior to Killarney; but we affirm that Lochs Lomond, Katrine, and Windermere – beautiful as they are – do not possess the various attractions of these comparatively small but most lovely lakes.

There is but one *lake* that we have visited which seems to us to be more beautiful in some features, and more sublime in others, than the Lakes of Killarney, and that is Loch Awe, at the foot of the mighty Ben Cruachan – the queen of all lakes for beauty – the monarch of all mountains for sublimity. The Lakes of Killarney are considerably smaller than Loch Awe; and even Mac Gillicuddy's Reeks, in all their vastness, are pigmies to Ben Cruachan; but though on a smaller scale, both lakes and mountains are only second to those wonders of Argyleshire, in the effect they produce upon the mind of the cultivated enthusiastic lover of nature. One great source of the beauty of the Lakes of Killarney is the number of islands upon them. From the windows of the inn can be seen at one view the promontory or Island of Ross, and the ruins of Rom Castle, the seat of the renowned O'Donoghue – the 'myth' of these parts – with whose name and fame almost every inch of ground is connected in some way or other, by history, tradition, legend, or song. In addition to this, covered with magnificent foliage, are Lamb, Heron, Cherry, Rabbit, Innisfallen Islands, O'Donoghue's Prison, and a score of others that become visible one after the other in rowing through the three lakes.

The Lakes of Killarney are three in number – the Upper, the Tore (or Middle), and the Lower; these, with their islands and other attractive objects, together with such matters of interest and importance as are to be met with in their immediate neighbourhood, we shall briefly describe.

The tourist, on approaching the Lakes, is at once struck by the peculiarity and the variety of the foliage of the woods that clothe the hills by which they are surrounded. The effect produced is novel and beautiful, and is caused chiefly by the abundant mixture of the shrub *Arbutus unedo* with the forest trees. The *arbutus* grows in rich profusion in nearly all parts of Ireland; but nowhere is it found of so large a size, or in such rich luxuriance, as at Killarney. On Denis Island there is one, the stem of which is 7 feet in circumference, and its height is in proportion, being equal to that of an ash tree of the same girth which stands near it. On Rough Island, opposite Sullivan's Cascade, is another fine specimen of *arbutus*, the circumference of which is 9 feet. It strikes its roots apparently into the very rocks, thus filling up spaces that would otherwise be barren spots in the scenery. Its most remarkable peculiarity is, that the flower (not unlike the Lily-of-the-Valley) and the fruit – ripe and unripe – are found

ECCLES' GLENGARIFF HOTEL CO. LTD.

IS strongly recommended by eminent Physicians for its equable, mild, but not relaxing climate. The excursions by land and water are numerous—amongst others, the celebrated drive to the LAKES OF KILLARNEY, thus described by LORD JOHN MANNERS :—

"The twenty miles from Kenmare to Glengariff form the *grandest road, barring the Alpine Pass, that I know.*"

The celebrated THACKERAY writes :—"*What sends picturesque tourists to the Rhine and Saxon Switzerland? Within five miles of the pretty Inn of Glengariff there is a country of the magnificence of which no pen can give an idea.* The journey from Glengariff to Kenmare is one of astonishing beauty, and I have seen Killarney since, and am sure that Glengariff loses nothing by comparison with this most famous of lakes."

From HAPPY THOUGHTS NOTES—*Punch.* " *Glengariff*—Eccles' Hotel. Charmingly situated. Facing the bay and on the road. Old-fashioned, covered with creepers and roses, and bed-rooms commanding the bay. Eccles' Hotel, Glengariff, is worth far more than a passing visit. I am delighted with it. It is, as far as attendance and cuisine and general comfort, the best hotel I've been in. The coffee-room seems to have been fitted up to the very latest fashion of taste; the climate is so mild that even at nine o'clock on an early spring evening you can sit out in front of the Hotel and enjoy your coffee and cigar."

MURRAY'S HANDBOOK FOR IRELAND describes this Hostelry as one of the best of the South of Ireland Hotels. Over Twenty Thousand Pounds have recently been expended on

THE ECCLES' HOTEL

and its extensive pleasure-grounds, through which are five miles of beautiful walks.

The Hotel is charmingly situated, and is replete with indoor comforts. Library, Billiard and Smoking Rooms, Private and Public Drawing Rooms, and Bedrooms, commanding a most lovely view of the Bay. The pier adjoins the hotel. Sea bathing, boating, fishing, shooting, etc. Reduced tariff during the winter months. Terms, and testimonials from Eminent Physicians, can be obtained from the Manager.

Above: Advertising handbill for Eccles' Glengariff Hotel. 'Charmingly situated. Facing the bay on the road. Old-fashioned, covered with creepers and roses, and bed-rooms commanding the bay. Eccles' Hotel, Glengarrif, is worth far more than a passing visit.'

at the same time, together on one tree. *Ross Castle* is built on a point of land which advances into the Lower Lake; and in the rainy season is insulated by the waters collecting from the Marsh. In summer, however, this peninsula (which the term Ross denotes) is connected with the island, as the castle is by a bridge and causeway. It is named Ross Island, and is the largest on the lakes. The castle is now in ruins, but a few years ago it had a military governor and a detachment of soldiers.

In Ross Bay is situated the boat-house. At the moment of embarkation the bugle is sometimes sounded, and an echo is heard as if proceeding from the castle, and more remotely from the slopes of Mangerton. This echo is the finest from the shores of the lakes, and is particularly beautiful if heard in the evening.

O'Donoghue's Prison is a steep rock, nearly 30 feet high, so called from a chieftain of gigantic stature, who is supposed to have consigned his enemies to this barren spot. His celebrated white charger has also a local record in another rock, resembling a horse, close to the Mucross shore, named O'Donoghue's Horse. To the north of O'Donoghue's Prison are Heron and Lamb Island; and further to the west is Rabbits, or Brown Island. Mouse Island, so called from its diminutive size, is a rock situated in the channel between Ross Island and Innisfallen.

Innisfallen is situated to the west of Ross Island, and is, as its name imports, a beautiful or healthy island. It has but two landing places, at one of which there is a Mole where tourists disembark. This beautiful spot consists of 18 acres of delightful woodland, knoll, and lawn. Among the curiosities pointed out to the visitors are – a holly, 14 feet in circumference; a hawthorn growing through a tombstone near the abbey; a crab tree, with an aperture, through which the guide recommends ladies to pass; and the Bed of Honour, a projecting rock, shaded by an old yew, and so called from having been visited by the Duke of Rutland, when he was Governor of Ireland. The *Abbey of Innisfallen* was founded in the sixth century, by A. Finlan, but the ruins now visible are evidently of a much later date. At the south-east corner of the island is an ancient Chapel, with a Saxon doorway; it is called the Oratory. The pasturage on this island is celebrated for fattening cattle.

The Upper Lake consists of about 720 acres, and is completely surrounded by mountains, which give it a sublime and picturesque aspect. Its extreme length is about 1¾ mile, but its breadth varies greatly. The principal islands on its surface are – Ronan, where parties occasionally dine; Duck; Mac Carthy's; Arbutus; Rossbarkie, or Oak, from the shores of which there is a splendid prospect; Knight of Kerry's; Eagle; and Stag. A fine view of the whole lake may be had from the Cramiglann, which rises from the brink of the lake in majestic grandeur.

Mucross Abbey adjoins the pretty village of Cloughreen, and is in the demesne of Henry A. Herbert, Esq., M.P., which includes the whole of the peninsula. The site was chosen with the usual judgment and taste of the 'monks of old', who

Above: Mucross Abbey was founded in 1448 as a Franciscan friary and has had a violent history, being ruined on numerous occasions. The friars were persecuted by Cromwellian forces and the Abbey is mainly in a ruinous state today.

Below: The Gap of Dunloe is a narrow pass between two mountains and contains five lakes. It was, and still is, a popular tourist destination.

invariably selected the pleasantest of all places. The building consists of two principal parts – the Convent and Church. The steeple of the church, between the nave and the chancel, rests on four high and slender pointed arches. The principal entrance is by a handsome pointed doorway, luxuriantly overgrown with ivy, through which is seen the great eastern window. The intermediate space, as indeed every part of the ruined edifice, is filled with tombs, the greater number distinguished only by a slight elevation from the mould around them. A large modern tomb in the centre of the choir covers the vault wherein, in ancient times, were interred the Mac Carthys Mor, and, more recently, the O'Douoghues Mor of the Glens, whose descendants were buried here as late as 1833. The dormitories, kitchen, refectory, cellars, infirmary, and other chambers, are still in a state of comparative preservation. A recess is pointed out as the bed of John Drake, a pilgrim, who, about a century ago, took up his abode in the Abbey for several years. As will be supposed, his singular choice of residence has given rise to abundant stories, and the mention of his name to any of the guides or boatmen, will at once produce a volume of the marvellous. The cloisters, which consist of twenty-two arches, ten of them semicircular, and twelve of them pointed, is the best preserved portion of the Abbey. In the centre grows a magnificent yew tree, which covers as a roof the whole area. It is more than probable that this tree is coeval with the Abbey, and was planted by the hands of the monks, who built the sacred edifice centuries ago. By visiting the 'Gap of Dunloe', and returning in a boat through the lakes, much of the sylvan beauty and the wild grandeur of Killarney may be seen in one day, should the traveller be pressed for time. But, whether his stay be long or short, the first excursion he should make is to this far-famed 'Gap'.

The attentive host and hostess of the Lake and Victoria Hotels will make all arrangements for his comfort. The usual mode of proceeding is to hire a car or pony, and ride half way through the pass; and thence proceed on foot over a shoulder of the Purple Mountain, to the head of the Upper Lake at Geragimene, where a boat will be stationed to row him through the three lakes. By this journey he will be enabled to see all the most celebrated and remarkable portions of the scenery; hear the finest and most renowned echoes; and learn from the civil, well-informed, and garrulous guides and boatmen, the legends, traditions, and histories of each spot he passes. The distance from the Victoria Hotel to the entrance of the Gap is from 4 to 5 miles, and the car proceeds about 4 miles through it, until it becomes too rugged or impracticable for vehicles or ponies. The traveller – who, if he be wise, will take a stout staff in his hand – must walk the remainder of the way to Geraghmene, at the head of the lake, a distance of about 4 miles more. We will not, by any general description of the scenery, anticipate the recital of the beauties that will enchant, or the sublimities that will enrapture him, during this excursion, but name each loveliness in its place, and dwell upon each sublimity in the due succession of its scenery.

The first point of interest on the road is the ruined Church and Round Tower of Aghadoe. These ruins stand upon a gentle eminence, from whence a very

Above: 'Irish Farmers at the Cattle Fair, Killarney, Ireland.' A very local scene depicted on a stereoscopic card published in 1905 by C. L. Wasson. These cards were a popular form of 3D photography using a pair of images taken a few degrees apart to mimic the action of the human eye. When seen through the special viewer the effect was striking.

good view of the lake is obtained. From this position the eye may wander over those delicious lakes and islands, and a mountain chain of 40 miles in length, stretching far beyond Mill Street, towards Cahirciveen and Valentia.

From Aghadoe to the entrance of the Gap of Dunloe, there is nothing to arrest attention. The Gap (for those who admire the wild, desolate, and sublime), is the most attractive portion of the scenery of Killarney. The entrance to it is abrupt and grand. The cleft between the mountains is supposed by the peasantry to have been caused by one blow from the weapon of one of the giants of the olden time, and is certainly magnificent enough to exercise a powerful influence over the minds of a much less imaginative people than the Irish. On the right of the winding road, Carrantual, and the kindred mountains, appear to look down upon the traveller from a height of more than 3,000 feet, affording no home but to the eagles; while, on the left, the scarcely less lofty peaks of the Purple Mountain and Tomies, raise their craggy heads above the clouds. That brawling river, the Loe, which gives name to the Gap, runs through it, expanding twice into gloomy lakes in the middle of the pass.

The Tore Cascade

The Tore Cascade, supplied from the 'Devil's Punch Bowl', in the mountain of Mangerton, is conveyed through a narrow channel called the Devil's Stream. It is a chasm between the mountains of Tore and Mangerton; the fall is between 60 and 70 feet. The path that leads to it, by the side of the rushing current which conducts it to the lake, has been judiciously curved, so as to conceal the full view until the visitor is immediately under it; but the opposite hill has been beautifully planted, art having been blended with nature and the tall young trees are intertwined with the evergreen *arbutus*, holly, and a vast variety of shrubs. As we advance, the rush of waters gradually breaks upon the ear, and at a sudden turning the cataract is beheld in all its glory.

The liberality of English tourists has accustomed almost all the poor people of the country to expect pennies and sixpences; and every now and then, in the traveller's progress through the gap, a little urchin, plump and good humoured, though shame-fully ragged, will pop up at the road side, and ask for 'a penny to buy a book!' or offer a tastefully made bouquet of heather and wild flowers to ensure the loose coppers or small coin of the Sassenagh. A little spring, a short distance from the gap, presents a scene of a different kind. A decent and comely-looking matron presides over the well, holding in one hand a wooden jug of goat's milk, and in the other a whisky bottle, and asks the traveller if he will not partake of her mixture. She strongly recommends it as the best of all preliminaries for a successful day among the mountains, and is usually surrounded by two or three nymphs of the same class as herself, all offering goat's milk and whisky, or, to those who prefer it, a draught of the clear cold water of the well, dashed with a due portion of the mountain dew, or national

Killarney

Left: College Street, Killarney, on market day. Donkeys were very much a part of Irish rural life. Cheaper than horses and hardier too, for the bog and wetlands of the interior, they were a common sight in every town and village at one point.

College Street, Killarney

This view, below, shows The Cooperage at Killarney. Note the barefooted children on the left. The cooper on the right is oblivious to the photographer.

The Cooperage Killarney

beverage. This matron, it appears, claims to be a Kate Kearney, the grand-daughter of the famous and veritable Kate Kearney,

'Who dwelt by the Lakes of Killarney',

and whose name is well known to all the lovers of Irish melody.

The echoes in the gap are very fine and distinct, and the guides being generally provided with a bugle, produce notes which are echoed back again by the Carrantual on one side, and the Purple mountains on the other; the latter passing them on to all the name-less hills in the vicinity, till the sounds die away in the dim distance – the effect is exceedingly beautiful. On firing a small cannon the mountains are immediately alive with sounds, hill thunders to hill – mountain peak to mountain peak – gorge to gorge – and rock to rock – until it seems as if contending armies were battling in the clouds.

At the end of the gap, a beautiful view presents itself, the Comme Dhur, or Black Valley, with its wall of mountains, and fair river meandering lazily through the flat meadows. The walk over the hill brings the traveller to Geraghmene, a beautiful cottage at the head of the Upper Lake. Here the boat despatched from the Lake or Victoria hotels is generally in waiting to receive the traveller, and convey him on his homeward journey through the Upper, Middle, and Lower Lakes.

The Upper Lake is, perhaps, the most beautiful of the three; although the charms of each are so varied, that it is difficult to accord the palm of superiority over her lovely sisters of any of these watery graces.

After the fatigues of the Gap of Dunloe the tourist appreciates the luxury of rest, and enjoys, sitting at ease, the delicious progress of the boat through the placid waters. The hills are clothed with verdure – the islands reflect their shadows in the lake – a heron occasionally wings its graceful flight over head – and the soft notes of the bugle die away amid the woody recesses of the hills. Every change of landscape is but a variety of loveliness. The first halting place is at the base of a magnificent hill, wooded to the very top, and called the 'Eagle's Nest'. At this spot the lake narrows to a river, and is in fact a stream connecting the Upper with the Middle or Tore Lake. The echo here is the most famous of all those of the lakes; and any traveller who, being in too great a hurry to get to the end of his journey, might refuse to linger here for a while, would be set down in the estimation of boatmen and guides as utterly deficient in respect for Killarney.

A mile beyond the Eagle's Nest is the old Weir Bridge, of two arches, one only of which is practicable for boats, neither is the passage at all times safe or pleasant. The current by which the Upper Lake discharges its surplus waters into the Tore Lake is exceedingly rapid, and it is customary for the tourist to disembark here, while the boatmen shoot the rapids. When the travellers re-embark the boat proceeds to the beautiful island of Denis, where persons who bring their luncheons or dinner with them from the hotel, can

GLENGARIFF.

VIEW FROM ROCHE'S ROYAL HOTEL, GLENGARIFF.

THIS HOTEL, commanding the finest view of the beautiful scenery of Glengariff, stands in its own tastefully-planted grounds, which slope to the water's edge, and have within their limits the romantic Glen and well-known Waterfall of Glengariff.

The internal arrangements are in accord with the extent of the establishment, and the requirements of a first-class connection.

Large Public Drawing Room, Billiard Room, &c.

Lawn Tennis, Boats, Carriages.

Special arrangements are made for families or others desirous of passing some time at the seaside.

Excursions to the Caves, and parties for Fishing, Sailing, and Shooting, personally arranged by the Proprietor. As a health resort Glengariff is now celebrated.

The Proprietor of ROCHE'S ROYAL HOTEL holds testimonials from some fifty of the most eminent medical authorities from all parts of the United Kingdom, Members of the British Medical Association, who stopped at this Hotel in the Summer of 1879.

The late Dr. MATTHIAS O'KEEFFE, A.M., M.D., Professor of Queen's College, Cork, wrote as follows :—" I cannot speak too highly of Glengariff as a healty resort, especially of Roche's Royal Hotel, surrounded as it is by its beautiful grounds, traversed by delightful avenues, and shaded by picturesque groves. Its southern aspect, and protection from north and north-east winds, render it a peculiarly desirable winter residence for invalids suffering from bronchial or other pectoral affections. The attention received, with the regularity and cleanliness of the hotel, cannot be excelled. To all this are added an admirable cuisine and cheerful society."

The Public Conveyances, in connection with the Cork, Bandon, and South Coast Railway, set down and take up passengers at the door of the Hotel.

WRITE TO THE PROPRIETOR.

Left: Another handbill for a hotel in Glengariff, this time Roche's Royal Hotel. 'Special arrangements are made for families or others desirous of passing some time at the seaside.'

Below: Suitably attired, a pair of gentleman travellers pause beside the Lakes of Killarney for beer and sandwiches.

be accommodated, at a snug cottage on the shore, with chairs and table, and a cook, who will dress salmon and potatoes, and supply hot water for whisky punch, for a small gratuity.

From this point to Glenn Bay is a delightful sail to another beautiful cottage, erected for the same purpose. The travellers are then in the large or Lower Lake, and within an hour's sail from the Victoria, and half an hour's sail from the Lake Hotel.

The Ascent of the Mangerton

The ascent of this mountain is usually made first, because its summit commands a very extensive prospect; and secondly, because, at a short distance from the top, a crater-like hollow on its side receives the waters of the hill, and collects them into a receptacle, famous all over the country for its odd name of the 'Devil's Punch Bowl'. The ascent commences at Cloughreen, a village about four miles from the Victoria Hotel. The inn at Cloughreen, called Noche's, or the Mucross Hotel, from its close proximity to that beautiful domain, is a beautifully situated and well conducted house, of which all travellers speak highly. Ladies and those travellers who do not like the fatigue of climbing on foot, may ride nearly the whole of the way up to the Devil's Punch Bowl.

The longer the tourist remains at Killarney the more lovely its mountains, valleys, placid lakes, and rushing waterfalls, appear. The weather, too, is often highly favourable for viewing the scenery under all its aspects. One day, in a clear and cloud-less atmosphere, the outlines of the hills stand sharply out against the deep blue sky, and the lakes lie silently and bright as sheets of burnished gold. On the day following, it may be wind and rain; then the high peaks of Carrantual and his sublime brothers of the 'Reeks', shroud themselves in the driving mists; the wind curls the broad bosom of the lake into foam-crested waves; and the clouds, from which, for one half-hour, rain in torrents may pour down, open in the next, and admit the sunshine into the magnificent landscape; the rainbow spans Carrantual and the Purple Mountains, then melting away into the heavy clouds upon which it was reflected, allows the whole of the glorious panorama to glitter in the full blaze of a midsummer sun. The effects on such a day are constantly changing and ever beautiful. The alternations of colouring, from the deepest dun, in which the lakes and mountains are enwrapped at one moment, to the grey, brown, purple, green, and gold, which girt them about with beauty in the next, are especially delightful to behold, study, and admire. Not only the grandeur, but the smaller features of the scenery are beautiful at Killarney. Under the splendid yew trees, hollies, and arbutuses of lovely Innisfallen, or amid the still more umbrageous foliage of Mucross, it is impossible to walk a step without discovering a new beauty in the landscape. Innisfallen alone offers almost every variety that can charm the eye and fill the imagination of the lover of nature. Those who delight in the shade of thick woods and countless wild flowers, may indulge here at sweet leisure. The lover of the pastoral glade, or

12017.—GLENGARIFF HARBOUR CO. CORK

Above: A colour view from Glengariff in County Cork. *(LoC)* 'We do not assert that the lake scenery of England and Scotland is inferior to Killarney; but we affirm that Lochs Lomond, Katrine, and Windermere – beautiful as they are – do not possess the various attractions of these comparatively small but most lovely lakes.'

the smooth-shaven lawn, sloping down to the water, may at a short distance find the scenery he admires; while he who delights most in rocks, mountains, and torrents, can, from the same little island, gaze undisturbed upon many of the grandeurs, and some of the sublimities of nature.

Tour from Killarney to Glengariff and Bantry Bay

From Killarney to Glengariff, a distance of forty miles by car, the road passes through scenery un-surpassed for beauty in any portion of the kingdom. For one third of the distance the lakes and mountains of Killarney continue in sight, and the tourist is enabled to acquire a still more intimate knowledge of them, in all their wondrous and lovely variations, than he can obtain even by sailing or roving about the lakes, or by coming down upon them from the heights of Dunloe or Mangerton. After passing Cloughreen, Mucross, and the splendid Tore Cascade (the music of whose rushing waters swells audibly upon the ear above the din of the car), the road winds round the shore of the Middle or Tore Lake, having the lake on the right hand, and on the left the Tore Mountain, clothed with the richest vegetation, and lifting his steep sides to a height of 1,760 feet. It then passes the connecting link of river between the Upper and the Middle Lakes, affording a fine view of the 'Eagle's Nest', the 'Purple Mountain', and high above them all, 'Macgillycuddy's Reeks', and 'Carrantual'. The road is a continual ascent all the way from Cloughreen, and, after passing the beautiful waterfall of Derricunihy (beautiful, though inferior to the Tore Cascade), reaches a point at which all travellers should halt for a while to survey the landscape around, above, and beneath them. This is the Police Barracks or Constabulary station. Standing here, or at any other point higher up the hill, a most magnificent view is obtained, including the whole of the lakes, the Gap of Dunloe, and Macgillycuddy's Reeks. Beyond this point, although Carrantual remains in sight the most conspicuous object in the landscape, there is little more to be seen of the lakes of Killarney. Let the traveller take his last look, and then prepare himself for a new panorama, as well worthy of his admiration as anything that he leaves behind him.

A ride of ten miles will bring him to the beautifully situated and picturesque town of Kenmare. The road descends gradually from the heights to the sea-level. Kenmare is built at the head of an arm of the sea. The Suspension Bridge across the 'Sound', is one of the greatest ornaments, as well as conveniences, of the town.

From Kenmare to Glengariff is a distance of seventeen miles. Were it thrice seventeen the tourist who loves the wild, the rugged, and the majestic scenery of the mountains, would think it short. The road attains a height from Kenmare of 1,000 feet above the level of the sea, with a gradual ascent of 150 feet in a mile. It passes through two tunnels – a rather unusual circumstance on any road, except railroads. One of them is 200 yards in length; and passing through it in the open car, the tourist will obtain, at either end, a view of the

12090. - VIEW FROM PORCH,
ROCHES ROYAL HOTEL,
GLENGARRIFFE, CO. CORK.

Above: View from Roche's Royal Hotel, overlooking Glengarriff Harbour, County Cork. See advertising handbill on page 64. *(LoC)*

Below: Postcard view of the Bere Island Ferry, Castletown–Berehaven, in Bantry Bay.

In Bantry Bay. Bere Island Ferry - Castletown - Berehaven.

hilly country which will make him wish that tunnels on common roads were somewhat more frequent. After passing the largest tunnel, which stands on the confines of Kerry, the road enters the county of Cork, and winds amid the rugged mountains of Glengariff to the sea, at the head of Bantry Bay.

The characteristics of Glengariff are wildness and sublimity. The name, which signifies the rough or rugged glen, has been well bestowed, and aptly describes it. Hitherto this unrivalled scene has been comparatively little known. A good hotel, or at all events, an inn of some kind was necessary to attract tourists, and this great want has been supplied. Let no tourist who loves nature in all her moods, the wildest as well as the softest, be deterred from visiting Glengariff by any doubt as to his creature comforts on the way. They will all be well and cheaply attended to; and leaving for awhile the better known districts of Scotland, Wales, and England, and the great continental high-ways of the sight-seers, he will be fully rewarded for his pains and selection. The mere repetition of the only possible epithets which admiration can apply to scenery fails to convey a proper idea to the minds of those who are not passionate lovers of it. All that the tongue or pen can do, is to affirm that it is 'magnificently beautiful'. No words can describe the beauty of some scenes. We can feel, but we cannot exactly explain our sensations. We can say no more of Glengariff than that it is both sublime and beautiful, and that it seems to us far better worth the time and cost of a pilgrimage than hundreds of other scenes of greater celebrity. The valley is three miles long, a quarter broad, and is shut out from the busy world by stupendous precipices. Through its entire centre flows in summer a peaceful stream, which in winter takes to itself the voice of many waters, and rushes a foaming torrent into the sea. The vegetation upon its banks is profuse and lovely, but it requires a residence of some days at Glengariff to become thoroughly acquainted with the beauties of this little river, and all the loveliness and grandeur that surround it. From the inn at Glengariff – which stands upon the shore of the Bay of Bantry – a different, but equally magnificent, prospect is obtained. The Bay stretches its broad, deep waters, studded with islands, towards the Atlantic Ocean. He who would see its beauties of island and of mountain in their full extent, should take a boat, on a fine summer evening, and be rowed across to Bantry. The distance is but nine miles, and the scenery is most superb. The picturesque island of Garnis crowned with a fort and Martello tower, erected shortly after the French made their appearance in the bay sixty years ago, is at first the most conspicuous object after leaving the inn; but as the boat proceeds on its course, the island and the fort dwindle into insignificance against the dark background of the lofty Glengariff mountains. As these seem to recede, the low island of Whiddy appears in front, with its solitary ruin of the ancient castle of the O'Sullivans; and the eye may range across the noble bay quite spell-bound with the beauty of the scene from the towering summit of Dade, or 'Hungry Hill', 2,100 feet high, to the thickly-wooded cove that leads to, and conceals, the town of Bantry.

Having now explored the beauties of Killarney, the tourist may continue his

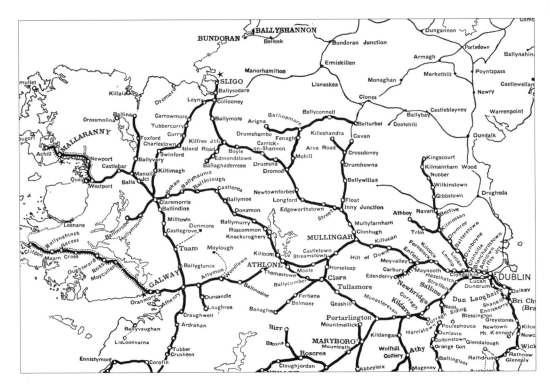

Above: A map showing the central railways of Ireland, published in 1906 by the Viceroyal Commission on Irish Railways. *Below*: The railway station at Maynooth, County Kildare, photographed in 1962. Maynooth is shown to the west of Dublin on the line to Sligo. It remains a very busy station as it serves two major educational establishments in the town. *(National Library of Ireland/wiki)*

railway course northward, via FARRANFORE, to the town of TRALEE. This forms part of a favourite route from Dublin to Killarney, *via* Limerick, Foynes, the Shannon, Tarbert and Tralee, for the accomplishment of which great facilities by way of return tickets are offered in the summer months.

MIDLAND GREAT WESTERN

Dublin to Blullingar, Athlone, and Galway

Leaving Dublin, we pass BLANCHARDSTOWN, and Clonsilla, close to the latter of which are *Clonsilla House*, the seat of R. French, Esq., and *Woodlands* (Col. T. White).

The Dublin and Meath railway runs out at this station, and unites itself with the Kells section of the Dublin and Drogheda line at Navan.

Lucan, situated on the Liffey, in a beautiful spot. It is a watering place of some note, and has a boiling spring and mineral spa. In the vicinity are *Lucan Abbey*, J. Gandon, Esq., the seat of Gandon, the architect; *Lucan House*, C. Colthurst, Esq.; *Weston Park*, J. Reed, Esq., near the Salmon Leap. Here races are held in February, March, June, and October. We then proceed to

Leixlip, situated close to the Salmon Leap. The Royal Canal is here crossed by an aqueduct 100 feet high. *The Castle*, the seat of Hon. G. Cavendish, was built by Adam Fitz-Hereford, and here King John lived when Earl of Montaigne. *Leixlip House*, seat of J. Nesbitt, Esq., is close at hand. Markets are held on Saturday; and Fairs May 4 and October 9.

MAYNOOTH
    A telegraph station.
    MARKET DAY – Saturday.
    FAIRS – May 4th, September 19th, October 9th.

Here are the ruins of the Geraldines' Castle, built in 1430. St Patrick's Roman Catholic College, a quadrangular edifice, containing chapel, rooms, and noble library of 18,000 volumes, covering 54 acres.

It was founded in 1795, and supported, until 1845, by a parliamentary grant of £3,900, since increased to £26,360 per annum. Close by is the princely mansion and domain of Ireland's *only* Duke (his Grace of Leinster), *Carton*, beautifully built, in Rye Water, erected by Casse's. It consists of a large centre, with wings. The dining-room is 52 feet by 24, and 24 high. Here is a splendid picture gallery, containing some of the *chef d'oeuvres* of Holbein, Claude, Poussin, and several Dutch masters. The grounds, park, etc., cover 1,000 acres. Queen Victoria visited here in 1849; and in 1855 one of the wings was partly destroyed by fire, when the Duchess narrowly escaped an untimely fate.

Passing KILCOCK, where markets are held on Wednesday; and fairs March 25, May 11, August 11, and September 29, we reach FERN'S LOCK, ENFIELD,

Cavan & Leitrim Railway

This 3-foot narrow gauge line opened in 1925 and it continued to run until March 1959. It survived mainly on coal traffic.

Above left: Lifting the tracks at Garadice, County Leitrim, in July 1959. *Left:* The demolition of Clones station, photographed in November 1960. *Above right*: Inside the C&LR workshop at Ballinamore, showing redundant locos being cut up. *(National Library of Ireland/wiki) Below*: The preserved Cavan & Leitrim Railway's depot at Dromod in County Antrim, 2007. Narrow gauge trains continue to run here. *(Sarah777)*

MOY VALLEY. HILL OF DOWN, and KILLUCAN, which has ruins of Hugh de Lacy's castle, and where fairs are held on March 27, May 25, September 29, and November 28, close to which is *Hyde Park*, seat of G. d'Arcy, Esq., we reach

MULLINGAR
A telegraph station.
MARKET DAY – Thursday.
FAIRS – April 6th, July 4th, August 29th, and November 11th.

This place has a large population employed in the wool and butter trade, and contains the ruins of two castles, and large infantry barracks for 1,000 men.

This station forms the junction of the line to Longford, which turns off to the right.

Mullingar to Cavan and Sligo

Multyfarnham, beautifully situated near Lake Deraveragh, has the ruins of an abbey, with a steeple 90 feet high, built in 1236, and which contains tombs of the Nugents. Here the Observantines held a chapter in 1529, and the Roman Catholics assembled in 1641. Fairs are held on March 4th, May 13th, September 1st, December 2nd. Close at hand are the beautiful seats of *Ballinadoon*, C. P. Murphy, Esq.; *Donore*, Sir P. Nugent, Bart.; *Mornington*, E. Daly, Esq.

From hence the line continues its course to CAVAN, a place of some importance, near to Lake Oughter; and from thence to Clones in connection with the Irish North Western.

We again proceed from Multyfarnham, in the direction of LONGFORD, and very soon enter the county of that name.

Longford, is only a small county, and returns two members. The general aspect of it is flat; but towards its northern extremity, where it projects into the counties of Leitrim and Cavan, its character varies, and the surface becomes rugged and uneven, partly consisting of good tillage ground, and partly of mosses and feus. A considerable quantity of linen is made in this county, and it is Improving and extending in all directions.

LONGFORD
A telegraph station.
HOTEL: Sutcliffe's.
FAIRS – March 25th, June 10th, August 19th, and October 22nd.
MARKET DAY – Saturday.

This is a small, though the principal, town of the county. It stands on the banks of the River Longford. It obtained considerable celebrity in an early age of history, on account of an Abbey, of which St John, one of the disciples

Vegetable Market, and Bridge over the River Shannon (E.), Athlone, Central Ireland. Copyright 1905 by Underwood & Underwood.

Athlone
Left: The vegetable market and the bridge over the Shannon at Athlone.

Mullingar
Below: Dominick Street in Mullingar. The county town of West Meath was connected to the railway network on 2 October 1848. The Midland Great Western from there to Dublin had opened in stages from 1846. The temporary station was replaced in 1851 with a more permanent structure upon the opening of the line to Galway.

DOMINICK STREET, MULLINGAR.

of St Patrick, was abbot. The castle of Longford has been the theatre of many interesting historical events, and belongs to the Pakenhams, Lords Longford, to one of whom the 'Iron Duke' was married.

SLIGO
A telegraph station.

A considerable town, situated at the eastern extremity of Sligo Bay; its population is about 15,000; trade – linen, flour, etc.; its harbour capacious, and will admit vessels of heavy tonnage. There are some interesting remains of an ancient monastery destroyed by fire in the year 1414, but subsequently repaired.

Midland Great Western Main Line continued

Leaving Mullingar we pass the station of CASTLETOWN, and in a few minutes arrive at STREAMSTOWN, the junction of a line to CLARA, a station in connection with the Athlone section of the Great Southern Railway to Killarney and Cork. Proceeding onward from Mullingar we pass the little station of MOATE, and soon after that of

ATHLONE
A telegraph station.
HOTEL – Rourke's.
MARKET DAYS – Tuesday and Saturday.
FAIRS – lst Monday after January 6th, 21st March, Wednesday before Ascension, 1st Monday in September.

A borough town, returning one member. The greater part is on the Westmeath side of the Shannon, which issues out of Lough Rea, a short distance north, but a portion is in Roscommon, on the opposite bank. The river flows over several rapids here, to clear which, a canal a mile long has been cut from the town to the lake. The houses are poor and dirty. Felt hats and woollen friezes are manufactured; and it enjoys a good carrying trade by steam and canal, as well as by rail; but its chief importance depends on its being a strong military post, commanding the ford over the Shannon, and the roads to the west of Ireland. To this end a castle was built here by Henry II, part of which remains, with later additions of great strength; it stood a long siege in the civil wars, and again in 1691, when General De Ginkell took it from the partisans of James II, for which he was created Earl of Athlone. James's commander, Col. Grace, was an old veteran, with whom the king had been very intimate. When summoned by De Ginkell to surrender, he fired his pistol in the air: 'These are my terms', he said, 'and when my provisions are gone, I will eat my boots.' He fell in the

Above: A motor-bus operated by the Midland Great Western Railway, on the Castlebar road from Newport, County Mayo, in western Ireland. Such vehicles were an important way of extending the railways' tendrils in rural areas. *(National Library of Ireland/wiki)*

Left: Ireland, despite its poverty, remained a playground for the aristocracy until the start of the First World War. Shown here is the local hunt at Loughrea *c.* 1905.

Bottom: Market Street, Castlebar. In the 1798 rebellion, with the aid of French forces, Castlebar was captured from the British army and the rout was known as the Races of Castlebar. A short-lived republic of Connacht was declared.

action, which was an easy one for the English, as Saint Ruth, the Irish leader, who was in the neighbourhood, neglected his duty to the besieged. He was killed a fortnight later, at the battle of Aughrim, 20 miles from this place (at Billcommadan Hill), where King James's supporters were finally routed. The castle includes barracks for 1,500 men, with an armoury, magazines, etc., altogether covering 14 acres. The ancient narrow bridge to the Leinster side, opposite it, is replaced by a new one of stone, built in 1644. On the old one was an inscription stating that it was erected by Lord Deputy Sidney (father of Sir Phillip), in Queen Elizabeth's time. *St Peter's* church stands on the site of an abbey, founded when the castle was first raised. From the battery of the latter is a view of the flat, boggy shores of Lough Rea, and *Moydrum Castle*, the seat of Viscount Castlemaine, is three miles off.

The Great Northern & Western Railway now turns off to the right. It intersects the counties of Roscommon and Mayo to Castlebar and will shortly be opened to Westport.

We then reach Ballinasloe, which is on the borders or the counties of Roscommon and Galway, and noted for its cattle fairs, which are held on the 5th October, May 7th, 4th and 6th July. The castle is an old, mated fort, of Elizabeth's time, and is the seat of J. T. Maher, Esq. There are markets on Saturday for corn. We reach

ATHENRY, where are the ruins of a castle and Dominican friary, built in 1261, by the De Birminghams. Markets are held here on Fridays, and fairs May 5th, July 2nd, October 20th, and Oranmore, where fairs are held on May 22nd and October 20th. A branch fifteen miles long, running to the right in a northerly direction forms a communication direct with Tuam.

ORANMORE – Here are the ruins of *Oranmore Castle*, built by the Earls of Clanricarde, on the site of which is *Oran Castle*, the seat of W. Blake, Esq., near the shallow and rocky bay of Oranmore. *Wallscourt*, Lord Waliseourt, and the round tower of *Murrough*, about 40 feet high, are close at hand.

Galway, a county in the province of Connaught, which returns two members, is bounded on the east by the River Shannon, the north-east by Roscommon, the west by the Atlantic, the north by Mayo, and on the south by Galway Bay. The general appearance of this county is remarkably beautiful, especially from the banks of the Shannon to the town of Galway. The soil is very fruitful; but agriculture is generally speaking, in a backward state. This county possesses both rivers and lakes in great abundance. Lough Corrib alone extends more than 20 miles in length, and eleven in breadth.

GALWAY

A telegraph station.

HOTELS – Midland Great Western Station, and Clanricarde Arms.

MARKET DAYS – Wednesday and Saturday.

FAIRS – May 31st, September 21st, and October 31st.

RACES in August.

IRELAND
LAND OF SCENERY AND ROMANCE —

BALLINAHINCH, Co. GALWAY

GREAT SOUTHERN RYS,

(IRELAND)
FOR PARTICULARS OF
TOURIST BOOKINGS, ETC.-
APPLY TO
P.J.FLOYD, TRAFFIC MANAGER
OR TOURIST AGENCIES

Galway

Top: Great Southern Railways poster for Ballinahinch, County Galway.
Above right: An early Edwardian photograph of the fishermen's cottages at the Claddagh, Galway. Fishing was a major industry for the city, as was spinning and weaving, traditional Irish cottage industries. A traditional Galway spinner is shown left.

BANKERS – National Bank of Ireland; Provincial Bank of Ireland; Bank of Ireland.

The capital of County Galway, a parliamentary borough, has a population of about 23,195, who return two members, and is a port in the west of Ireland, at the head of a fine bay. A small stream, three or four miles long, serving as the outlet to Lough Corrib, runs through the town into the harbour, which contains a floating dock of five acres, and has good anchorage outside. This is proposed to be the starting point for America, the run to which would be lessened about 350 miles.

Galway was founded in the 11th and 12th centuries by the Twelve Tribes, as they were called, consisting of the Burke, Blake, Joyce, D'Arcy, Lynch, Skerrett, and other families, several of whom still flourish – the Blakes for instance, represented by the Marquis of Clanricarde, so named after *Richard de Burgh*, who built the town wall, 1235, of which a gate or two remains. The great statesman and orator was a branch of this family. Beautiful black Connemara marble, one of the chief products, is sawn and polished at Franklin's mills. Fish provisions, and a little paper also exported. Formerly there was a good trade in wine with Spain, which produced an infusion of foreign blood on this side of Ireland, where the round olive face and Spanish complexion may be frequently noticed. Many houses in Old Town, which belonged to merchants, yet retain, outside, their armorial bearings and moorish carvings, and are built in the Spanish style within. Lynch's house in Lombard Street, or Deadman's Lane, is an example; the crest is a *lynx*. The ancient cross-shaped church, with its spire, was built in the 14th century; in former times the living was a wardenship, independent of the bishop, which the tribes elected. On Clare River is the new *Queen's College*, a handsome Elizabethan quadrangle, by Sir J. Deane, opened in 1840; it is 275 feet by 215, and has a tower 110 feet high. The *Claddagh*, is a suburb, where the fishermen and their families live, exclusively, to the number of 5,000 or 6,000; their market being close to an old tower and gate. They are peaceable and clean, but superstitious, never going out to fish, nor allowing others to go out, except on lucky days, and are governed by their own laws and customs, under a 'king' or admiral, chosen annually.

The noble bay, which is seven miles across, opposite the town, widens to 23 miles at the mouth, where the Arran Islands form a natural breakwater, and abounds with excellent harbours. On the Great Arran is a revolving light, 500 feet high; and from here, they tell you, Hy Brysall, the old Irish paradise, can be seen 'on a clear day'. At all events, America, a more sober and useful paradise, is not far off.

In the neighbourhood of Galway are, *Men'o Castle*, seat of Sir V. Blake, Bart.; *Roscom Round Tower*; *Loughcooter Castle*, Viscount Gough's seat, near the Slieve Doughty Mountains, 1,280 feet high: *Aughrim*, where De Ginkell defeated the forces of James II, 1691; *Tuam*, and its modern Roman Catholic cathedral; but the most interesting excursion is that to...

Achill
Top left:
Roundstone,
Connemara,
c. 1950.

Achill Sound Achill Island.
Co. Mayo.

Middle left:
Achill island is
the largest island
off the coast of
Ireland. At the
time of Bradshaw,
the island was
not connected
to the mainland,
but the bridge
shown here was
built in 1887 and
has been replaced
twice since then,
the latest bridge
dating from 2008.

The Sound Hotel, Achill Island

Bottom left:
The Sound Hotel,
Achill island.

Connemara and the Killeries

A trip of 35 or 40 miles; or, 90 miles, if extended through Mayo to Westport; through a grand country of lakes and mountains, with noble coast scenery, washed by the Atlantic. It was called the 'kingdom' of Connemara, a word which means, 'bays of the great sea', and till lately belonged to one or two proprietors, the first of whom was Colonel Martin of Ballynahinch. 'He once boasted to the Prince of Wales, to put him out of conceit with Windsor Park, that the avenue to his hall door was thirty miles long.' The fact being that it was the only road in the county, and ended at Ballynahinch – Hall's *Ireland*. The women dress in homespun scarlet cloaks, and spin all day long. It is now settled by various new proprietors, and is in course of being reclaimed and cultivated. Here is the chief scene of the evangelical reformation, under the blessing of God in progress, of the devoted Bishop of Tuam and his Irish preaching clergy.

From Galway the road goes along Lough Corrib to Oughterard, 16 miles, past *Aughaanarc*, an old seat of the Flaherties, and a vast collection of Druid stones spreading two miles; whence, by Maam Ture Inn, through Joyce's country, to Leenane, in the Killeries, is nineteen more. The Maam Inn, under a mountain 2,000 feet high, commands a fine view of the lake, with another of the Flaherties' Castle in the distance. From Oughterard, by Ballynahinch to *Clifden*, is 14 miles. Clifden, is a beautiful mountain town, on an inlet, founded by the D'Arcys, about thirty years ago, and is the centre of the new reformation. Its late proprietor sold all his estates, and is now one of the most active of the working clergy here. In the neighbourhood are the Twelve Pins, or Peaks, the highest of which is 2,930 feet. Following the coast road to Leenane, 30 miles, you come to Ballynakill Harbour, Kylemore Pass, a grand thing to see; and Salruc Pass, is grand, in the Killeries, which is a narrow, but splendid, sea inlet, between high and picturesque mountains, like a Norwegian fiord (Inglis). Then to *Leenane*, near *Delphi*, the beautiful seat of the Marquis of Sligo. This round may be extended by following the equally bold and wild county of Mayo, to Newport, Westport, and Achill, another Protestant settlement, where some of the cliffs are 1,500 to 2,000 feet, sheer down to the sea, or to the mountains round Clew Bay, 2,600 feet high, and more, at Croaghpatrick and Mulrea; and in Tyrawley.

Dublin, Wicklow, and Wexford

Wicklow – The greater part of this county, which returns two members, is mountainous. Towards the interior this Alpine region is boggy, uncultivated, and rendered additionally cheerless in the want of wood; but throughout a long extent of its borders, and particularly on the sea coast, it assumes a splendour and variety of scenery not to be surpassed in any part of the island. The mountains and rocky elevations are here magnificently bold, and the country is plentifully clothed with ornamental wood. Agriculture is still in a backward state, though considerable improvements have been recently introduced.

Left: A Connemara colleen on a period 1900s postcard. One does wonder today if tourists went to look at the locals and view them as primitive savages, much in the way they went to Africa and did the same. In total contrast, the main street of Bray, shown above, looks like any other town in the United Kingdom at the turn of the twentieth century.

Bottom left: On the last Sunday of every July, a pilgrimage is made to Croagh Patrick, with a Mass being offered.

Bottom right: At the vale of Avoca, there were mines producing copper and lead. Bradshaw mentions them but is more concerned with the meeting of the waters to be found here.

Passing DUNDRUM (has remains of an old castle), STILLORGAN, (has Darley's extensive brewery, and close at hand Stilloryan Park, H. Verschoyle, Esq., *Stillorgan House*, H. Guinness, Esq.; *Redesdale*, Archbishop of Dublin), CARRICKMINES (has ruins of an old castle) and SHANKILL (the hill is 912 feet high), we reach

BRAY

A telegraph station.

HOTELS – Quin's and Queen's.

MARKET DAYS – Tuesday and Saturday.

FAIRS – January 12th, March 1st, May 1st and 4th, July 15th, August 5th and 20th, September 14th (for friezes), December 4, (for cattle).

This town, which is most beautifully situated, has remains of a castle (now used as barracks), and a race course. Here is a pretty lake, and a river abounding with trout. Close at hand are Kilhuddery, near the Sugar Loaf, seat of the Earl of Meath. *Bray Head*, which commands an extensive view, G. Putiand, Esq.; *Old Court*, Major Edwards, *Old Connaught Howe*, Lord Plunkett, near which are the ruins of a castle, and coins have been found.

On arriving at *Bray* we pass *Kilruddery*, Earl of Meath's seat, up the famous Dargle Glen, to *Powerscourt*, the seat of Viscount Powerscourt, and *Tinnahiuch* belonged to Grattan. Glen of the Downs, near Delgany, under the Sugar Loaf Peaks, the highest 1,650 feet. Devil's Glen, fall of 100 feet, near Ashford on the Vartry. *Wicklow Castle* (31 miles from Dublin), on to *Arklow Castle*, built on a basalt cliff at the Avoca's mouth. Up the Avoca, by *Sheldon Abbey* (Earl of Wicklow), to the Wooden Bridge and Avoca inns, at the Second Meeting of the Waters (viz., the Aughrim and Avoca), from which a path may be taken to the left, past Aughrim, under Croaghu Kinshela (a granite peak, 1,935 feet high) to Drumgoff inn, and Lugnaquilla, the highest point (3,039 feet) of the Wicklow Mountains, in a wild and rugged spot, at the Slaney's Head. But the usual course is from the Second Meeting, up the 'Sweet Vale of Avoca', past the Copper Mines, to the First Meeting of the Waters (the one alluded to by the poet), at the junction of the Avon-beg and Avon-more, under Castle Howard. By the Avon-more (3 miles) on to Rathdrum (11 miles from Arklow) and Laragh Bridge, to Glendalough, or Glen of the Two Lakes, in a desolate hollow of the mountains (2,100 to 2,500 feet high), the seat of an early bishopric, with St Kevin's Bed (a hole in the cliff), parts of cathedral, church, etc. (destroyed by the Norman invaders), and a round tower 110 feet high. Thence you may take the road over Wicklow Gap, or pass, 1,560 feet high, to the head of King's River, down to Poul-a-phonea Fall, on the Liffey round to Dublin. Or by the direct route from Glendalough, to Lough Dan and Tay, on the Annamoe, near *Luggelaw* (the Latouches' seat), under Djouce Mountain (2,384 feet) and other peaks, on to the two Loughs Bray at the top of Glencree, by Sally Gap pass

Wicklow & Wexford Railway
Above: On 9 August 1857 the Enniscorthy to Dublin train was derailed on a timber viaduct at Bray Head. Two people were killed in the accident, another twenty-five injured. The Wicklow & Wexford Railway had opened two years earlier, engineered by Isambard Kingdom Brunel to follow the difficult coastal route.

Drogheda
This was the location of the Boyne Monument, placed here after the battle and destroyed by explosives in 1923.

and Enniskerry to Dublin. Since the Rebellion, the Wicklow Mountains are traversed by good military roads; the highest parts are bare, but the lower well fringed with wood. on which account Swift compared the district to a 'frieze coat, edged with gold lace'.

WICKLOW

A telegraph station.
HOTEL – Byrne's. MARKET DAY – Saturday.
FAIRS – March 28th, May 24th, August 12th, and November 23rd.
Races in May.
BANKERS – National Bank of Ireland.

This town, the capital of the county of the same name, has a population of about 2,798, who are employed in the copper and lead ore trade. It contains a church, with round mound, three chapels, race stand on the Murrough, ruins of an Abbey founded by the O'Byrnes in Henry III's time, barracks, etc. It stands on the sea coast, at the mouth of the River Leitrim, which was once defended by a fortified rock called the *Black Castle*. It is now, however, a place of but little strength in a military point of view, and of slight commercial importance, as it has no manufactures. The bay is much exposed to south-easterly winds, which render the neighbouring coast very dangerous. Two lighthouses have been erected, 208 feet high, with fixed lights.

GLENEALY and RATHDRUM stations.

DUBLIN AND DROGHEDA

The first station on this line is Raheny, in the neighbourhood of which are *Raheny House*, J. Sweettnan, Esq.; *Raheny Park*; *Killested Abbey*, D. Nugent, Esq.

The nest station is the JUNCTION of the

HOWTH BRANCH

We are no sooner clear of this than the train is announced at
BALDOYLE, situated on an isthmus leading to the Hill of Howth. It is a pretty bathing-place, but its harbour is very shallow, suited only for small boats.

HOWTH

A telegraph station.
HOTEL – Royal.
BOATS to and from Ireland's Eye. Tariff – 2s, including all charges.

Malahide

'This place is celebrated for its oyster fisheries, and has an old church, with ancient tombs of the Talbots, and in the churchyard some beautiful old Chesnut trees. Close at hand is Malahide Court, the princely seat of Lord Talbot de Malahide, built as a square castle, with round corner towers, and contains a noble hall, with oak carvings, altar-piece by Durer, a gallery of portraits, and pictures by Dutch and Italian artists.'

Howth

Below: 'Howth has risen within a very few years to a considerable degree of importance by the construction of a magnificent harbour for the protection of vessels bound for the port of Dublin.' An 1890s view of the harbour and Ireland's Eye.

Howth is the name of a peninsula on the coast of Ireland, which forms the northern boundary of the bay of Dublin. On the northern side of this peninsula stands the town of Howth, which has risen within a very few years to a considerable degree of importance by the construction of a magnificent harbour for the protection of vessels bound for the port of Dublin. It consists of two piers, erected by Rennie at a cost of £800,000, which project for a considerable distance into the sea; one is rather more than 2,493 feet from the shore, and the other 2,020 feet: the entrance is 300 feet wide, and the area enclosed within this vast mass of masonry exceeds fifty English acres. The fixed light, built in 1818, is 43 feet high, and can be seen 11 miles distant. On landing at the harbour of Howth, the first object that attracts the attention of the traveller is a ruined abbey, which directly fronts him. Placed on a precipitous bank, considerably elevated above the water's edge, and surrounded by a strong embattled wall, it may be considered half temple, half fortress. It contains a fine tomb of a knight and lady. In the castle, Lord Howth's seat, are the old Abbey Bells, Tristram's sword, a picture gallery in which is a portrait of Swift. On Bally Point there is an immense fixed light, erected in 1813, 114 feet high, and visible 15 miles at sea.

Dublin and Drogheda Main Line continued

Passing PORTMARNOCK, where are ruins of Rob's Wall Castle, built by the De Birminghams, church at Carrickhill, and two Martello towers, we arrive at

MALAHIDE
A telegraph station.
HOTELS – Royal, Railway.

This place is celebrated for its oyster fisheries, and has an old church, with ancient tombs of the Talbots, and in the churchyard some beautiful old Chesnut trees. Close at hand is *Malahide Court*, the princely seat of Lord Talbot de Malahide, built as a square castle, with round corner towers, and contains a noble hall, with oak carvings, altar-piece by Durer, a gallery of portraits, and pictures by Dutch and Italian artists. The line traverses the harbour on a wooden viaduct of eleven spans, each 50 feet wide.

DONABATE, a living which was held by Pilkington, the author of *Dictionary of Painters*, who was born at the seat of C. Cobbe, Esq., *Newbridge*, in 1730, the collection of pictures at which was selected by him. Close at hand is *Turrey*, the old seat of the Barnewell family (Lord Trimlestown), whose tombs are in the old church.

RUSH and LUSK. The former has a pier harbour, defended by a Martello tower. *Rush House*, the seat of R. Palmer, Esq., contains a fine gallery of old masters, and many antiquities, especially vases from Pompeii: and the latter place contains the east end of the Abbey Church, with fonts, and effigies of

Laytown Races

Above: Race-goers pour off the train at Layton station on their way to the Laytown Races in County Meath, *c.* 1910. The station opened in 1844 and was renamed Laytown & Bettystown in 1913. *(National Library of Ireland/wiki)*

Red Island, Skerries, Co. Dublin.

Skerries

Red Island was the first purpose-built holiday camp in Ireland. Located at the Skerries, it had 250 centrally-heated bedrooms and was connected to the mainland by a causeway.

Sir C. Barnwell, W. Dermot, J. Birmingham, square steeple, stone-roofed crypt, with round turrets at three corners, and a round uncapped tower on the fourth; close to which is *Kenmure*; the seat of Sir R. Palmer, Bart., with an old church, with camp and Martello towers close at hand.

SKERRIES

Telegraph station at Malahlde, 8¾ miles.
MARKET DAY – Saturday. FAIRS – April 23, August 10.
MONEY ORDER OFFICE at Balbriggan, 4 miles.

It has a pier harbour and Holmpatrick Church, and is celebrated for the landing of Sir P. Sidney in 1575.

Meath – A great part of this maritime county is occupied by valuable pasture grounds, divided by verdant banks; and the general aspect of the country may be described is that of an undulating. rich and highly cultivated plain. The farms are often very extensive, but the farm houses, except when they belong to large proprietors, are in general wretched huts; and the houses of the humbler classes are nothing but md hovels. Yet the mansions of the nobility and gentry are numerous throughout every district, and in several instances are spacious and splendid. The ecclesiastical structures of past ages, venerable and picturesque in all the varied stages of decay, abound in nearly every part of the county; and in their vicinity are still remaining several ruinous crosses of elaborate workmanship.

BALBRIGGAN

A telegraph station.
MARKET Day – Saturday, for corn.
FAIRS – April 29, September 29.

This place has a population of about 2,959, who are chiefly employed in the stocking, linen, tanning, muslin, and embroidering trades. The harbour is inside a pier 600 feet long, with a fixed light 35 feet high, visible 10 miles distant. The Carjee Half Tide Rock lies one mile N. E.; and *Hampton Hill*, the seat of E. C. Hamilton, Esq., is close at hand.

Then passing GORMANSTON (near which lies *Gormanston Castle*, Viscount Gormanston), and LAYTOWN, we arrive at

DROGHEDA

A telegraph station.
HOTEL – Imperial.
MARKET DAYS – Fridays and Saturdays.
FAIRS – March 10, April 11, May 2, June 22, August 26, October 29, November 21, December 19.

Boyne Viaduct, Drogheda

The Boyne Viaduct
Carrying the Great Northern Railway's main line between Dublin and Belfast across the River Boyne, the viaduct was designed by the Irish engineer Sir John Macneill and completed in 1855.

Top left: The original straight iron girder sections shown on a postcard, *c.* 1905.

Middle left: It was refurbished in the 1930s with new steel girders, and the two tracks were reduced to a single track.

Below: A recent view of the viaduct. *(Trounce)*

BANKERS – Branch of Bank of Ireland, Provincial Bank of Ireland, Branch of Hibernian Joint Stock.

A parliamentary borough in the county of *Louth*, on the Boyne, one member, population about 16,880. Cotten and linen yarn is spun. It enjoys a good trade in Irish produce, and has remains of two old monasteries and St Lawrence's town gate, a Tholsel or assize court, linen hall, and various other buildings, Including the cathedral of the Romish diocese of Armagh, whose primate resides here. Small craft can come up to the quays from the sea, which is six miles below.

Two or three events serve to render the town memorable. Here Lord Deputy Poynings held a parliament in 1496, which enacted 'Poynings' Law', establishing the supremacy of English rule. It was given up to storm by Cromwell in 1649, in revenge for the Irish massacre of 1641, when 100,000 Protestants were put to death. He breached the wall from Cromwell's Fort which commands the town. His career in Ireland is still remembered in the saying, 'May the curse of Cromwell be on you'. And on the 10th of July, 1690, the famous battle of the Boyne took place, when William III utterly defeated the Jacobite party. It was fought at *Oldbridge*, three miles above the town, and a pillar on a rock 150 feet above the picturesque banks of the river marks where Schomberg (William's general) fell, in his 82nd year. William was in the thickest of the contest and narrowly escaped being shot. James II stood at a safe distance from his gallant Irish on Donore Hill, commanding a view of the field; he slept at *Carntown Castle*, the night before, and William at *Ardagh House*. Two elms mark where Caillemote, the leader of the French Protestant auxiliaries, was buried. Sheephouse Farm was a point strongly contested by both parties. 'Change leaders', said the beaten Irish, 'and we will fight the battle over again', but their despicable sovereign made off as fast as he could to Dublin, where he met the Duchess of Tyrconnel. 'Your countrymen run well, madam', he said. 'Not quite so well as your majesty,' said the lady, 'for I see you have won the race.' William of Drogheda, and Miles, were natives. Near at hand is the *Grange*, J. Maguire, Esq.

Hibernia, one of the first steam locomotives in Ireland, was designed by Richard Roberts of Manchester.

Drogheda

Above: In Drogheda, Lord Deputy Poynings held a parliament in 1496, which enacted 'Poynings' Law', establishing the supremacy of English rule over Ireland.

Above: As with the rest of the United Kingdom, there were numerous strikes in Ireland in the first decade of the twentieth century. Here, soldiers protect a train. By 22 September 1911, Dublin was down to two days' food supply.

KELLS BRANCH

Drogheda to Kells and Oldcastle

DULEEK has a fine stone cross and old church. Fairs are held here on March 25th, May 3rd, June 24th, October 18th, and close at hand are *Drogheda House*, Marquis of Thomond; *Somerville*, Right Hon. Sir W. Somerville, Bart., M.P.; *Athcarne*, De Batte's seat, and *Plutten*, J. D'Arcy's; and BEAUPARC, with *Beauparc House*, the seat of J. Lambert, Esq.

NAVAN

A telegraph station.

HOTEL – Morans.

MARKET DAY – Wednesday.

FAIRS – Easter and Trinity Mondays, Second Monday in September, 1st Monday in December.

This town, which was an important military station in Edward the Fourth's time, has a population of about 6,898, who are engaged in the provision, flax, flour and paper trades; has some fine cavalry barracks, a church with an old tower, Athlumney Castle, in ruins, and close at hand *Boyne Hill*, the seat of Lieut. Col. J. Gerrard; then passing BALLYBEG, we arrive at

KELLS

Telegraph station at Navan, 9¾ miles.

MARKET DAY – Saturday.

FAIRS – February 27, May 27, July 16, September 9, October 16, November 17.

The church contains tombs of the Marquis of Headfort's family, whose castle, with an old cross and round tower 99 feet high, are close at hand.

Louth. One of the smallest counties in Ireland, returns two members. It abounds in those rude vestiges of antiquity which consist of earth-works, chiefly designed for sepulchral purposes, or acting as places of defensive habitation. Cromlechs, and other relics of anti-Christian ages, although much lessened in number within the last century, are still numerous, and in several instances extremely curious. There are also many remains of ecclesiastical and military structures.

VIROLICIA ROAD

Oldcastle, a market town on the River Crosswater, deriving its name from a Castle which once occupied the site. Limestone is abundent in the neighbourhood.

DUBLIN AND BELFAST JUNCTION

Drogheda to Dundalk and Newry

DUNLEER: here fairs are held monthly.

  CASTLEBELLINGHAM has ruins of the old castle of the Bellinghams, destroyed at the battle of the Boyne, and *Castlebellinghan House*, Sir A. E. Bellingham, Bart. Fairs, Easter Tuesday, and October 10th.

DUNDALK

  A telegraph station.
  HOTEL – Arthur's; Imperial.
  MARKET DAY – Monday.
  FAIRS – Third Wednesday in every month, except the 17th of May.
  BANKERS – Branch of Bank of Ireland, Branch of National Bank of Ireland.

A borough and seaport town in the county of Louth, returning one member. It is situated on the banks of a river of the same name, at the mouth of the Irish channel. It is a place of some traffic, from which considerable quantities of corn are annually exported. The manufacture of cambric, which forms part of the trading pursuit of the inhabitants, was first established here in 1737.

  Passing MOUNTPLEASANT and JONESBOROUGH, at the latter of which places Fairs are held on June 4th, August 15th, October 21st, and December 4th, we arrive at

From here the line going up to Belfast continues through Northern Ireland.

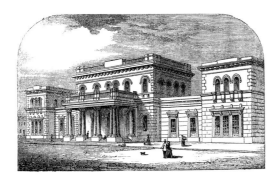

Above: Belfast's Great Victoria Street station. See page 104.

Opposite: Railway posters have been used since the 1830s to encourage travel on the railways. This chromo-lithographed poster was issued for the Donegal Railway Company at the end of the Victorian era. It is typical of the early railway posters, with every element of the line thrown on the sheet, but later posters would be much simpler and by the inter-war years the posters had become works of art by recognised artists and designers.

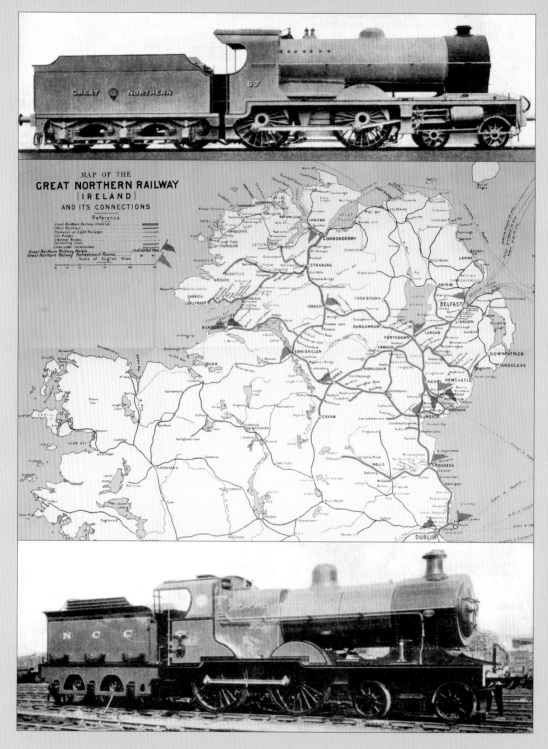

Centre: Map showing the Great Northern Railway's network in Northern Ireland. *Top*: *Kestrel*, a Great Northern Railway 4-4-0 passenger loco of the V class. *Bottom*: Another 4-4-0, this time in the service of the Northern Counties Committee, later part of the LMS.

Northern Ireland

> Distance from station, 3 miles. A telegraph station. HOTEL – Drausfiehrs.
> STEAMERS to and from Liverpool twice a week. Fares 10*s* and 3*s*. Return
> Tickets, available for 14 days, 15*s*. MARKET DAYS – Tuesday, Thursday, and
> Saturday. FAIRS – April 3rd and October 29th.

This town has a population of about 26,000, who return one member, and
are employed in the iron and brass foundries, tanneries, linen, and glass
manufacturers. It is situated close to the Newry mountains, which rise 1,385 feet,
and contains the ruins of a monastery, with a yew tree planted by St Patrick,
founded in 1237, by Maurice M'Loughlin; a castle built by Sir J. De Courcey, and
destroyed by Bruce in 1318. It has a considerable coasting trade, but only small
vessels can approach the Quay, all larger vessels being obliged to discharge their
cargoes at Warrenpoint, six miles below it.

GORAGH WOOD station.

POYNTZPASS, so called from Sir T. Poyntz having forced his band through the
Pass, has ruins or a castle which commands its entrance. Fairs are held here 1st
Saturday in every month. Acton church; close at hand are *Acton House,* R. Dobbs,
Esq.; *Acton Lodge*, P. Quinn, Esq. (the descndant of Sir T. Poyntz); *Drumbanagher
Castle,* Colonel Close; and TANDERAGEE (which has Tanderagee Castle, built on
the site of O'Hanteris Castle), the Duke of Manchester. Markets on Wednesday,
and Fairs 1st Wednesday in every mouth, July 5th, and November 5th.

NEWRY, WARRENPOINT, AND ROSTREVOR

> Telegraph station at Newry, 6 miles. HOTEL – Royal: new, clean, and
> comfortable; conducted on English principles.
> FAIRS – Last Friday in every month.

This is one of the most picturesque and romantically situated watering places
in Ireland, and consequently much frequented. It occupies a very pretty site
on Narrow Water at the head of Carlingford Bay, and on the line of the Newry
Navigation. It contains a church, built by R. Hail, Esq., of Narrow Water Castle, in
1805; a Roman Catholic Chapel, Presbyterian and Wesleyan Chapels, etc., etc.

> Distance from station, 2½ miles. Telegraph station at Newry, 8½ miles.
> MARKET DAY – Saturday. FAIRS – Shrove Tuesday, August 1st, September
> 19th, November 1st, and December 11th.

Right: The Merchant's Quay at Newry, which had become a port in 1742 when it was linked by canal to Lough Neagh. *(National Library of Ireland/wiki)*

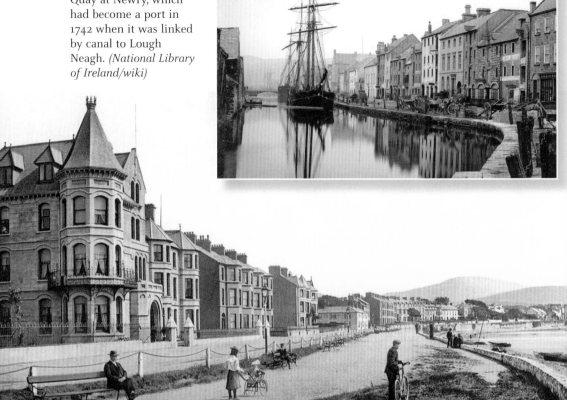

Above: The Esplanade at Warrenpoint. Bradshaw described the town as 'one of the most picturesque and romantically situated watering places in Ireland'. *(LoC)*

Left: Church Square in Monaghan with St Patrick's, the Monaghan Parish Church, in the background. *(Jacobethan86)*

This is a pretty and fashionable watering place in Carlingford Bay. It contains remains of Castle Rory, built by the Dungannons; a granite obelisk to General Ross, some salt works, which employ the greater portion of the 690 inhabitants. Close by is *Rostrevor Lodge*, D. Ross, Esq.

Dublin and Belfast Junction Main Line continued

PORTADOWN

A telegraph station. HOTEL – Manchester Arms.
MARKET DAY – Saturday. FAIRS – Third Saturday in the month, Easter and Whit-Monday.

This town has a population of about 2,560, engaged in the linen trade. Here are ruins of a castle given by Charles I to Obyns and which belongs to the Duke of Manchester. Close at hand is *Ballyworkan*, seat of G. Pepper, Esq.

Armagh, which returns two members, is beautifully diversified with gentle hills; the soil is rich and fertile, except in the district called the Fewes, which is exceedingly mountainous, but even a considerable part of this rough tract has been brought into cultivation. Throughout the county, however, the farms are in general small. The linen manufacture in all its branches flourishes here, and, indeed, forms the chief employment of the inhabitants.

ULSTER

Clones to Armagh and Belfast

Taking our departure from CLONES and in a direction parallel with the Ulster Canal, the little village of Smithborough associated in some measure with the manufacture of spades, shortly presents itself. A distance of about 4 miles further brings us to the town of

MONAGHAN

A telegraph station. HOTELS – McPhilips' and Campbell's.
MARKET DAYS – Monday (for linen and pigs), Tuesday, Wednesday, and Saturday, (for grain). FAIRS – 1st Monday in every mouth.

This town was built by the Blaneys in 1611, and has a population of about 3,484, who are principally shop-keepers. Large flour mills are in the vicinity. The Ulster canal passes the town. Its public buildings consist or a county court house and jail, cavalry barracks, fever hospital, and workhouse. Close at hand are the ruins of some forts. *Cortalvin*, Lord Rossmore; *Castle Shane*, Right Hon. E. Lucas; *Camla Vale*, Colonel Westenra.

GLASSLOUGH, TYNAN, and KILLYLEA stations.

LMS NORTHERN IRELAND
by Hesketh Hubbard V·P·R·B·A·R·O·I·

Above: Great Northern Railway 4-4-0 Compound No. 86, *Peregrine*, near Portadown, County Armagh. This was one of five locos built for the GNR by Beyer Peacock, Manchester, named after birds of prey.

Left: LMS poster showing Cushendall on the Antrim coast road. The LMS was the only one of Britain's 'Big Four' railway companies to operate rail services in Northern Ireland.

Bottom left: GNR advertisement for three of the company hotels, at Rostrevor and Warrenpoint in County Down, plus Bundoran in County Donegal.

A telegraph station. MARKET DAYS – Tuesday, Wednesday, and Sat. FAIRS – May 21st, June 10th, August 12th, Tuesday before Oct 10th, and November 20th. BANKERS – Branch of Bank of Ireland; Branch of Belfast Banking Co.; Branch of Northern Banking Co.; Branch of Ulster Banking Co.; Provincial Bank of Ireland.

This is the seat of the primacy of Ireland and a city, returning one member. It is well seated on Druira Sailech, i.e., Willow Hill, near the Callan, and originated it is said, in a church and college founded by St Patrick, in 435, which became a celebrated school of learning. Some writers, indeed, go back to a royal city called Eamania, and a palace of the Ulster kings, three or four centuries before Christ, but this is fabulous. After suffering from war and other contests, in which it was burnt about seventeen times, it was reduced to a mere heap of cottages, when Dr Robinson (Lord Rokeby) succeeded, in 1765, to the primacy, and began to renovate it. To this munificent prelate it is indebted for some of its best buildings and endowments, such as the Palace, a quiet looking pile, 90 feet long, with beautiful gardens, open to the public, a chapel, some abbey ruins, and a column of 157 feet, built as a memorial to the Archbishop's friend, the Duke of Northumberland; the College, or royal school, near the Mall; a public lending Library, close to the cathedral, with 14,000 vols., from which any one within 30 miles may borrow — besides a reading-room in the Tontine Buildings. A well-organised Observatory on a hill 110 feet high, north of the college, containing transit zenith-sector, mural circle, telescope, Electro-Meter, etc.; assembly rooms, the county Infirmary, besides barracks, shambles, and bridges. To these Primate Beresford added a Fever Hospital, and Primate Stewart the Market-house.

The Mall is a well kept walk, near the Deanery, about 1,500 feet long. At one end is the Court House, built in 1809, of the coarse marble quarried here, with a Grecian portico, etc. The County Jail is near it. A Lunatic Asylum was built in 1825, for £20,000, on the Ballynahone ruin, not far from the town. Armagh is now, through the liberality of various primates of the see, one of the prettiest towns in Ulster. Most of the houses are of stone, with slated roofs. There are linen halls for the sale of the staple produce of the district, with corn mills, tanneries, etc., and five banks, one of the latter being built on the site of a monastery, founded in 610, by St Coltuab. A Weslyan chapel stands where John Wesley often preached. St. Mark's church is modern.

On top of the hill, on the site of St Patrick's wooden church is the Cathedral, which was rebuilt in 1675, in the shape of a cross. It is only 183½ feet long, or less than many English parish churches; but it is yet one of the largest in Ireland, which has few grand ecclesiastical buildings to show, except those that are picturesque ruins. Armagh Cathedral has been lately restored by Cottingham (the restorer of St Alban's church), chiefly at the cost of the present primate, Lord J. Beresford, whose total subscriptions for this object have amounted to £30,000. There is a bust of the excellent Archbishop Robinson, by Bacon, and

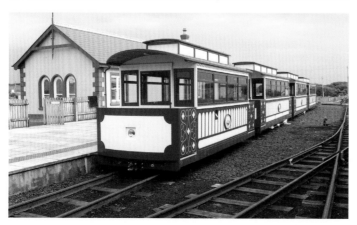

Above: 4-4-0 No. 174, *Carrantuohill*, hauling a passenger train near Portadown.

Left: Northern Ireland Railways (NIR) Class 4000 at Great Victoria Street station in June 2013. The NIR is a government-owned company formed in 1968, when it took over the Ulster Transport Authority which had operated the province's trains since nationalisation in 1948. *(Gillet's Crossing)*

Bottom left: The Giant's Causeway & Bushmills Railway is a narrow gauge line on the County Antrim coast. Only 2 miles long, it began life as the longer Giant's Causeway Tramway in 1883, operating between Portrush and the Causeway. *(Infogcbr)*

other monuments by Rysbrach, Roubiliac, and Chantrey. Brian Boru was brought here to be buried after the battle of Clontarf. Not far off is the Roman Catholic cathedral, a handsome building in course of erection; works in abeyance, (1859).

The ecclesiastical province of Armagh takes in one half of Ireland (the other half belonging to Dublin), including six dioceses. That of Tuam was an archbishopric before 1834, when it was suppressed; hence the Romish Dr M'Hale's boast, that he is the only Archbishop of Tuam.

One of the most distinguished holders of the primacy was the learned and pious Usher or Usther, whose family name (like the Butlers, Grosvenors, and others), originated in an office held about court by its founder. Usher came to the primacy in 1624, and retained it through good and evil report till episcopacy was abolished, and Charles I brought to the block. He had the anguish of witnessing his sovereign's execution from the leads of Wallingford House (now the Admiralty), at Charing Cross; and commemorated the day by fasting and prayer, till his death, which happened at his friend Lady Peterborough's, at Reigate. A love of books, a sweet temper, and a quiet firmness of principle, were the chief traits in this amiable prelate's character.

In the neighbourhood are various objects of notice, such as Navanrath, said to be the real site of Eamania; Crieve Roe — Nial's grave, where a King of Ulster was drowned in 846; Dobbin's Valley, a beautiful cultivated hollow; the Vicar's Cairn; *Castle Dillon*, seat of Sir T. Molyneux, Bart.; Hamilton's Baun, i.e. a fort, about 60 feet square, the scene of many cruelties in the massacre of 1641, and on which Swift wrote some lines. The county has a cultivated and prosperous appearance.

RICHILL (where Fairs are held on Shrove Tuesday, July 26th, October 15th).

PONTADOWN Junction.

PORTADOWN, DUNGANNON, AND OMAGH JUNCTION

Portadown to Dangarnon and Omagh.
ANNAGHMORE, VERNESBRIDGE, TREW, and MOY stations.

DUNGANNON

A telegraph station. MARKET DAYS – Monday (grain), Thursday (linen, cattle, provisions). FAIRS – 1st Thursday in every month.

The spirit of improvement manifest here, by its being the place of residence of the Earl of Lurgan, speaks greatly in his favour.

We now pass the stations of DONAGHMORE, POMEROY, CARRICKMORE, SIXMILECROSS, with its ruins of Glenawley Castle, and BERAGH, arriving at

Omagh, by the junction with the Londonderry and Enniskillen Railway.

Top left: York Road station is also referred to as Belfast York Road station. Opened in 1848 for the Belfast & Ballymena Railway, it saw a major rebuild in the 1980s. It closed in 1922 and no traces of the station building remain. *(National Library of Ireland/wiki)*

Lower left: Great Victoria Street, the Great Northern Railway company's station in Belfast, *c.* 1900. It was originally opened by the Ulster Railway Company on 12 August 1839. *(National Library of Ireland/wiki)*

Below: Looking down the Royal Avenue in the heart of Belfast, viewed from Castle Junction in pre-automobile days, *c.* 1895. Even the trams are horse-drawn. *(LoC)*

Ulster Main Line continued

LURGAN, which had a castle burnt in 1641, and rebuilt in 1690, and where Markets are held on Fridays, and Fairs the 2nd Thursday in every month, August 5th, and November 22nd.

MOIRA

Here is Moira Castle, the seat of the Hastings family, and the birth place of the first Marquis, the gallant Earl Moira, grandfather of the lamented and amiable Lady Flora Hastings, whose melancholy demise has cast an indelible stain on the British Court of the nineteenth century. Fairs are held on the 1st Thursday in February, May, August, and November. Markets on Thursday. We then arrive at

LISBURN

A telegraph station. HOTEL – Mrs Loinoti's.
MARKET DAY – Tuesday. FAIRS – July 21st and October 5th.

LISBURN, 8 miles from Belfast, up the Lagan, is a pretty thriving seat of the linen trader (population about 6,384), which was first introduced by the French Huguenots (Protestants), driven out of France in 1685, by Louis XIV's revocation of the Edict of Nantes. The present court-house was their chapel. Near Two Sisters' Elms are traces of a castle, built by the Lord Conway, who founded the town in 1627. Lisburn House seat of Earl of Lisburn, at whose seat, Golden Grove, in Wales, Jeremy Taylor found shelter in the civil wars, and wrote some of his best works. He died here in 1667, and is buried, in Blaris church, (as also is Lieutenant Dobbs, who was killed in action against Paul Jones in 1778), which is the parish church of Lisburn, and the cathedral of Down diocese; it is marked by an octagonal spire. Bishop E. Smith was a native. Here are large damask and thread and flax-spinning factories.

Passing DUNMURRY, where are the remains of walls, and *Dunmurry House*, the seat of W. Hunter, Esq., we arrive at BALMORAL, and soon after at

BELFAST

A telegraph station. HOTELS – Imperial; Royal; Commercial; Queen's and Plough. CARRIAGES and CARS at the station and hotels. Tariff – 1s per hour (driver included). OMNIBUS FARES between Commercial Buildings, Botanical Gardens, and Queen's College, once hourly, from 9 a.m. to 7 p.m., 2d; Castle Place, York Street, and the Ballymena railway station, 2d; Commercial Buildings, Great Victoria Street and the Ulster railway station, 2d; Commercial Buildings, Queen's Quay, and the Belfast and County Down railway station, 1½d. STEAMERS – See, Bradshaw's Guide.
MARKET DAY – Friday. FAIRS – August 12th and November 8th for horses.

Above: RMS *Titanic* and RMS *Olympic* were the first two of a trio of ships built for the White Star Line, the third being RMS *Britannic*. Only one of the three completed a fare-paying passenger voyage, with *Titanic* sunk mid-Atlantic and *Britannic* (shown here on the stocks) in the Aegean, while being operated as a hospital ship. *Below*: Propellers of the *Olympic* in the dry dock. The *Olympic* was launched on 20 October 1910. *Titanic* followed on 31 May 1911 and sank on 15 April 1912 after striking an iceberg on her maiden voyage. *Britannic* was not launched until 1914 and was converted to a hospital ship, before being sunk by a mine in November 1916. (LoC)

This is the great seat of the Irish linen trade, and the capital of Ulster, in Antrim county, at the mouth of the Lagan, where it falls into Belfast Lough, on a flat situation, among hills, which at Divis, rise into a fine mountain peak, 1,513 feet high. Though ranking the second port in Ireland, it stands first for manufactures and trade, returning one member. The tall chimneys and factories for spinning linen and cotton yarn are the most conspicuous buildings; none of the churches are worth remark; in fact Belfast is a modern town, scarcely going back beyond the last century. In 1805, the customs' duties were only £3,700, but in 1846, upwards of £360,000, while the registered tonnage of the port amounted to £62,000. The first graving dock was constructed in 1795, but since 1839 very great improvements have been made in the harbour, a deep channel having been cut right up to the town, so that large vessels drawing 16 or 18 feet water, which used to stop at Carmoyle, are now able to dischargo cargo at the new quays, which with splendid docks, etc., have cost the corporation half a million of money. The rates also are low, and the consequence is that the tonnage inwards and outwards nearly doubled. The lighthouse stands on screw piles, worming down into the sand and rock. There are building slips for vessels of 1,000 tons, beside foundries, machine factories, fifty spinning mills, weaving factories, dye and bleach works, provision stores, etc.

The staple manufactures include damask, diapers, drills, cambrics, plain and printed linens, and handkerchiefs of all kinds; among cotton goods are velvets, fustians, jeans, gingham, quilting, embroidery, calico printing, etc. A society for encouraging flax growing in Ireland was established here in 1841; and there is an excellent School of Design. Goods are sold at the white and brown (or

Below: Underwood & Underwood stereoscopic card showing the SS *Oceanic* under construction at the Harland & Wolff works in Belfast. Taken immediately prior to the launch, she was painted in an all-over grey to make her easier to photograph.

un-bleached) Linen Halls, which Queen Victoria inspected on her visit to the town in 1849. The Commercial Buildings, in the Ionic Style, were built in 1822. At the Literary Society is a good museum; the Botanical Society possesses a garden on the river, where an island of 20 acres has been laid out with shrubberies.

Belfast is honourably distinguished for its literary exertions, and abounds in schools and societies for the promotion of education as well as of arts and letters. Here Dr Edgar began the temperance movement as early as 1828. Besides the Academy, founded in 1786, and the Royal Academical Institution, founded in 1810, both of a collegiate character, there is the new Queen's College, established under Sir R. Peel's Act, a handsome Tudor pile, 300 feet long, built by Lanion, and opened in 1849. Benevolent societies of all kinds are numerous.

Out of fifty churches and chapels (the Presbyterian being nearly one half), the visitor may notice St Ann's, with a copper roof and wooden spire, and the Grecian portico of St George's, which originally belonged to a palace, begun by Lord Bristol (a free thinking bishop of Derry), at Ballyscullion. The palace of the Bishop of Down is here. One of the four chapels is the Roman Catholic Cathedral of Down.

It was at Belfast, and not till 1704, that the first English Bible published in Ireland, was printed. A handsome bridge (Queen's Bridge), on five arches, built

Above: Postcard of the Palm House at the Botanic Gardens on Stranmillis Road. Designed by Charles Lanyon and built by Richard Turner, the glasshouse was completed in 1840 and pre-dates those at Kew (also by Turner) and Paxton's Crystal Palace of the Great Exhibition.

in 1841, crosses the Lagan (besides two others) to the suburb of Ballymacarrett, in county Down. Formerly there was a long straggling bridge, 2,560 feet, which many a weary traveller must have found to be a bridge of size indeed. The Bay or Lough in which Belfast stands is a fine roomy channel, 15 miles long, and 3 to 6 broad. An excellent view of it is obtained from Mac Art's Fort, on the top of Cave Hill, a basalt peak, 1,200 feet high, 3 miles north-west. The stone quarried here is carried down to the harbour by a tram rail. Near it is White House factory, where Mr Grimshaw built the first cotton mill in Ireland, in 1784.

It was from this place that John M'Cormac, Esq., a native, sailed to the Western Coast of Africa, from whence he was the first to introduce the Teak timber, of which so many ships of war have been and are still constructed in the British Government Dock Yards.

Within a few miles are *Ormeau*, the seat of the Marquis of Donegal, chief landed proprietor here; *Belvoir*, Sir R. Bateson, Bart.; and a vast Druidical remain, called the Giant's Ring, in the centre of which is a cromlech, or Druid's altar. Divis Mountain had a small observatory fixed there by the Ordnance survey, till a storm carried it away. When Drummond's light was first exhibited in 1826, on Slieve Snaght in Donegal, it was seen here, though 66 miles distant. Cave Hill commands a fine view.

BELFAST AND COUNTY DOWN

Belfast to Newtownards & Downpatrick

Down, a maritime county, bounded east and south by the Irish sea, returns two members. Its surface is extremely irregular; in some parts mountainous and hilly, in others level and flat. The highest mountain is Slieve Donard, which rises 2,800 feet above the level of the sea. Woods and forests are found in various parts, and taken as a whole, the county may considered both productive and beautiful. There are several mineral springs here, but the chalybeate ones arc the most numerous. The principal employment of the inhabitants is in making of linen and muslin; the bleaching is carried on to a considerable extent on the banks of the river Bann.

Passing KNOCK, DUNDONALD, and COMBER, the latter of which has an old castle, Druidical rowans, and a church, built on the site of an old abbey. Fairs, January 14th, April 5th, June 28th, and October 19th, we arrive at

NEWTOWNARDS, a town of muslin weavers and embroiderers, belonging to the Londonderry family, at the head of Lough Strangford, which is a lagoon full of islands, with nothing notable about it except Grey Abbey. 'Will Watch, the bold smuggler', flourished at Newtownards.

At **Bangor**, 5 miles north of Newtownards, a pretty bathing place, in the mouth of Lough Belfast, is the castle of Lord Bangor. The name is derived from the Bean choir or white (i.e. stone) church, built here in the 12th century,

Top left: Even though the main Irish gauge was 5 feet 3 inches, the Northern Counties Committee also had 64 miles of 3-foot track, in addition to 201 miles of broad gauge. Shown here is a narrow gauge 2-4-2 on a broad-gauge transshipment truck in Belfast.

Middle left: One of four special diesel rail cars built for the GNR at their Dundalk works.

Bottom left: The 'Rail Omnibus', a pneumatic-tyred vehicle operated on the GNR. The wheels had steel rims between the rubber tyres and the rails. The advantage claimed for this design was that the train could act more like a bus, stopping and picking up passengers at level crossings, thus offering an economical service for more sparsely populated districts.

when stone churches were more uncommon, instead of the wooden buildings, attached to an ancient monastery here. *Ballyleidy* belongs to the Lord Dufferin; the Dowager Lady Dufferin is a grand-daughter of Sheridan, and the author of a beautiful poem. *Crawfordsburn*, seat of the late Sharman Crawford, Esq., the great advocate of tenant-right; here there is a customary charge of £5 to £20 an acre, paid by the incoming tenant to his predecessor, for the good will as it were, on the ground of improvements. Most of the people in the lowlands of this county are of Scottish descent. The railway is new open to Donaghadee harbour, whence a submarine telegraph was laid down in 1853, across to the Scottish coast. In front of the harbour are the Copeland Islands, near which, before a lighthouse was built, the *Enterprise* sunk in 1801; she was loaded with dollars, a part of which was afterwards recovered by Bell in his diving apparatus.

Retracing our steps to the junction at Comber, we pass on, via BALLYGOWAN and SAINTFIELD to BALLYNAHINCH and the city of

DOWNPATRICK
A telegraph station. MARKET DAY – Saturday.
FAIRS – First Saturday in each month.

Situated on the river Quoile, in a valley, at the south-west corner of Strangford Lough, has a population of about 5,000, and returns one member to, parliament. The Cathedral contains the tomb of Lord Kehany; the window at the east end is worth notice.

Belfast to Holywood
Passing SYDENHAM and TILLYSBURN, we arrive at

HOLYWOOD
A telegraph station. HOTEL – Power's.
MARKET DAY – Saturday. FAIRS – Every three months.

Holywood, or Hollywood, is a pretty bathing place on the Lough, 5 miles from Belfast, where the Irish Presbyterians signed the Solemn League and Covenant, 1644. The church is on the site of a priory, from which the name of the place is derived.

Antrim – A maritime county in the province of Ulster, returns two members. The principal towns are Belfast, Lisburn, Carrickfergus, Antrim, and Ballymoney. The chief employment of its inhabitants is the manufacture of linen, and the flax extensively grown; and many of the farmers are weavers. Their farms seldom exceed a few acres in extent. The county is in some parts mountainous and barren; the richer and more fertile districts lay towards the south.

The Tubular Bridge.
The Gobbins.

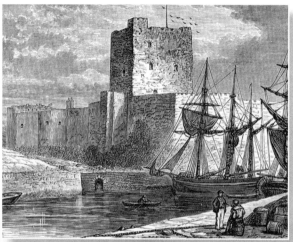

Above: A postcard of a tubular bridge on the Gobbins Path in Islandmagee, County Antrim. This cliff pathway was built by the engineer Berkeley Deane Wise.

Left: 1823 engraving of the castle at Carrickfergus.

Below: The railway viaduct at Canlough in County Antrim, with the town hall on the right and the post office on the left, *c.* 1900. *(National Library of Ireland/wiki)*

BELFAST AND NORTHERN COUNTIES

From Belfast we pass the stations of GREENCASTLE, WHITEABBEY, and JORDONSTOWN, and arrive at the Junction of the

CARRICKFERGUS BRANCH

In the course of five or six minutes after passing the station at TROOPER'S LANE, the arrival of the train is announced at

CARRICKFERGUS

Distance from station, 1 mile. A telegraph station. OMNIBUSES to and from the station. MARKET DAY – Saturday. FAIRS – May 12, November 1.

A seaport town in the county of Antrim, situated on a bay called Belfast Lough, or Carrickfergus Bay, its name signifies the Rock of Fergus, from an Irish chieftain Fergus, who was drowned here. A castle built by the De Courceys, on the site of this fort, still exists, with its two towers, and walls nine feet thick; it commands the harbour below, in which King William landed in 1689, on his Irish campaign. Parts of the town walls are left.

The town was once the principal seaport of the north of Ireland, but its trade his been for the most part transferred to Belfast: the fishery in the bay employs a great portion of its inhabitants, and many others are occupied in spinning and weaving. It is a principal depot for military purposes. Bishop Tennison was a native. Close at hand are *Thonfield*, P. Kirk, Esq.; *Glyn Park*, Captain Skinner.

The line continues via WHITEHEAD, BALLYCAREY and BALLYLIG, to

LARNE

From whence steamers ply regularly across the channel in connection with the trains of the Portpatrick Railway at Stranraer.

Larne has a Castle; Edward Bruce landed here in 1315. Much lime is sent from thence to Scotland. Agnew Mountain, 1,560 feet high, lies to the left. The pedestrian who has four or five days at his command would not grudge the time occupied in taking a tour along the coast from this plan to the Giant's Causeway, a description of which is given on page 120.

Belfast and Northern Counties Main Line continued

Passing BALLYNURE (here Fairs May 16th, September 5th, and October 25th), BALLYCLARE and DUNADRY stations, we reach

ANTRIM

A telegraph station. HOTEL – McMatly's.
MARKET DAYS – Tuesday and Thursday. FAIRS – January 1st, May 12th, August 1st, November 12th. BANKERS – Ulster Banking Co.

Ireland's Round Towers

Many theories have been put forward concerning the purpose of the Irish Round Towers. From their Irish name, *Cloigtheach*, meaning 'bell house', it is thought they were most probably built as belfries.

Top: The Drumbo tower (1843).

Left: The towers at the Rock of Cashel *(Jermey Keith)* and at Devenish Island beside Lower Lough Erne. *(Swedish National Heritage Board)*

Below: Painting of tower and abbey ruins at Devenish, *c.* 1916.

This small town, which gives name to Antrim county, stands at the mouth of Six Mile Water, as it falls into Lough Neagh, has a population of about 6,000, whose trade consists of paper, linen, etc. All this part of Ireland once belonged to the O'Neils or O'Nials; and in the petty contests which took place between them and the settlers planted over their heads by James I, Antrim had a full share. The last historical event was the death of Lord O'Niell, who was mortally wounded, in an action with the rebels of 1798, though the latter were defeated. St Patrick, the missionary and church-builder, founded a church here in 495, which the present structure replaces. There is nothing remarkable in it, but close at hand is a perfect Round Tower, 95 feet high, well worth examination. There are about eighty of these singular towers in Ireland, of which about one third are perfect.

They are from 60 to 130 feet high and only 8 to 11 feet in diameter; being shaped in general like the Eddystone Lighthouse. Each story is lit by a single window; and the -whole pile is surmounted by a cap or conical roof.

From the absence of any authentic early history of Ireland, it is difficult to account for their origin. Whether they were built by the Irish, or the Danes, whether for Christian or pagan uses, is a keen subject of dispute with antiquarians – each of whom, like Smith O'Brien Esq., would 'die on the floor' for his favourite theory, and would, probably perish of ennui if the question were satisfactorily settled. Those in existence are always found to be near a church or abbey; and human bones have been discovered at the bottom of some. Dr Petrie, the best informed of Irish writers on this fertile theme, thinks they were built for belfries, and also storehouses in cases of attack. The square keep of Norman castles, and the peel towers on the Scottish border were designed for a similar purpose, and are built on much the same plan.

Lough Neagh, the largest lake in the United Kingdom (nearly 100,000 acres, 60 miles in circuit), is a fine sheet of water. At one period it was surrounded by immense forests, the fallen timber of which process of ages has been converted into coal and lignite, in which cornelian and other pebbles are found. This lignite, which is a common production in certain localities,, gave rise to a story that 'the waters of the lake were petrifying'; while the stumps of trees seen at the bottom have been magnified into the 'round towers of other days' of Moore's song. There are three small islands, and the Bann is its only outlet. As it is not more than 102 feet in the deepest part, the time may come when this immense basin of useless water will be drained, like the lake of Haarlem. Two miles from Antrim, on the west side of the bay, towards Randalstown, is *Shane's Castle*, the seat of the O'Neill's, but now owned by the Rev. Mr Chichester.

A small feeder of the lake, Maine Water, runs through the grounds, which are large and well planted. The castle itself was burnt in 1816, and is a picturesque mill; a small house near it is now occupied by the family. The castle is supposed to be haunted by the Banshee, whose wail is heard whenever one of the O'Neills die. This is firmly believed. A bloody or red hand is the arms of Ulster, from the

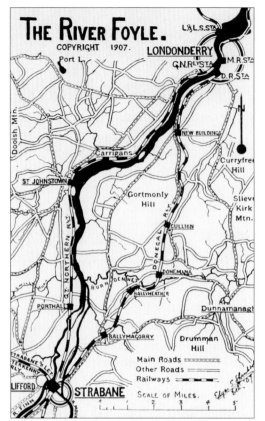

Londonderry Airs

County Londonderry is also known as County Derry, and likewise Derry is preferred by the nationalists as the name for the city itself. The railway had arrived at the Waterside station in 1852.

Left: From the guidebook of the Great Northern Railway, *c.* 1906, a map showing the line from Strabane to Londonderry.

Above: The First Presbyterian Church.

Below: A view across the Foyle showing the 1863 Craigavon bridge. The old wooden bridge was wrecked by an iceberg in 1862.

story that 'the first O'Neill was one of a company, the leader of which promised that whoever touched the land first should have it. O'Neill, seeing another boat ahead of his, took a sword, cut off his left hand, flung it ashore, and so was first to touch it.' This hand appears in the arms of all baronet's dignity, created by James I, at the plantation of Ulster. Within a short distance are *Antrim Castle*, the seat of Viscount Massareen; and *Castle Upton*, the ancient Elizabethan seat of Lord Templetown.

COOKSTOWN JUNCTION.

COOKSTOWN BRANCH

RANDALSTOWN

Telegraph station at Antrim, 5¼ miles. HOTEL – O'Neill's Arms.
MARKET DAY – Saturday. FAIRS – July 16th, November 1st.

This place, which was burnt by the rebels in 1798, bas a population of about 1,300, employed in cotton spinning and weaving; Barracks, Market House, five Chapels, and Dispensary.

Passing the intermediate stations of STAFFORDSTOWN, TOOME, CASTLEDAWSON, MAGHERAFELT, and MONEYMORE, we arrive at the terminus of the branch at

COOKSTOWN

Hotels – Commercial; Stewart's Arms. MARKET DAYS – Tuesday and
Saturday. FAIRS – First Saturday in each month.

This town contains about 4,000 inhabitants, who are chiefly employed in the linen trade. In the vicinity is *Killymoon*, now in the occupation of Mr Cooper (Saxon style, designed by Nash, who built Derryloran church), owner of the town. *Lissan*, seat of Sir T. Staples, Bart. There are also some forts and other remains to be seen.

Belfast and Northern Counties Main Line continued

BALLYMENA

A telegraph station. HOTEL – Ainsworth's.
MARKET DAY – Saturday, for linens.
FAIRS – July 26th, August 21st.
BANKERS – Provincial Bank of Ireland; draw on Spooner and Attwoods.

Here are the ruins of an old castle, founded by the Adairs, which the rebels held in 1798. The town has a population of 6,000, principally employed in the linen trade.

Portrush

Top left: Ballymena–Portrush railway, opening at Portrush station on 4 December 1855. It is the last stop on the Coleraine–Portrush line, where passenegers connect with trains to Derry, Belfast and beyond.

Lower left: Postcard view of the Northern Counties Hotel in Portrush.

Below: A Colorchrom view of the seafront. The town's proximity to the Giant's Causeway made it a popular destination for tourists in the late nineteenth and early twentieth century. The tramway began in Eglinton Street alongside the station. See page 102.

Londonderry – The general appearance or this county, which returns two members, is mountainous and barren, but the soil in the vallies is very fertile. A range of mountains running from the northern coast, the whole length of the county, in a southern direction, forms the principal ridge in the county. This mountainous region consists of wild Alpine tracts, uplands covered with heaths and rough gravelly basaltic eminences. Londonderry is particularly rich in its mineral products, which if properly worked would give employment and opulence to its inhabitants.

BELLAGHY – Monthly cattle fairs are held, and in the vicinity are *Bellaghy House*, J. Hill, Esq., and *Bellaghy Castle,* H. Hunter, Esq.

BALLYMONEY – Fairs are held on May 6th, July 10th, August 10th, and markets on Thursdays; it has a population of about 4,000, who are engaged in the linen and butter trade. Close at hand are *Leslie Hill*, J. Leslie, Esq., *O'Hara Brook*. C. E. O'Hara, Esq.

COLERAINE

A telegraph station. HOTEL – Clothworkers' Arms.

MARKET DAYS – Monday, Wednesday, Friday and Saturday, for grain.

FAIRS – May 12th, July 5th, November 3rd.

BANKERS – Provincial Bank of Ireland.

A borough town, with a population of about 5,857, who return one member, and are employed in the salmon and eel fisheries, and manufactures of paper, soap, candles, and leather, situated on the banks of the river Bann, about three miles from the sea. A sand bank extends across the mouth of this river, and prevents its navigation by vessels of heavy tonnage in rough weather. The town is large and handsome, and contains a church built in 1614, with old tombs, which stands on the site of the priory and old abbey. Close at hand is mount Sandel, 200 feet high; *Down Hill*, Mrs. Maxwell; *Dundoun House*, J. Boyd, Esq. Archbishop Vesey was a native.

Passing PORTSTEWART (a small bathing place, of which Dr Adam Clarke, the commentator, was a native) and to whom a monument has just been erected, (1859), we arrive at

PORTRUSH

A telegraph station. HOTEL – Coleman's.

MONEY ORDER OFFICE at Coleraine, 4 miles.

This small, yet pretty bathing place, which has Dr Adam Clarke's School and monument, and where the mirage is often seen, is beautifully situated on a basalt peninsula, opposite the Skerries Rocks, and has an excellent view of the ...

Above: A UNESCO World Heritage Site since 1986, the Giant's Causeway remains one of the most popular attractions in Northern Ireland. *(Man vyi)*

GIANTS CAUSEWAY

The railway being now completed to Portrush, an easy access is opened to this remarkable place, which by no means ought to be lost sight of. To those who have time, a most picturesque tour along the coast from Carrickfergus, about 64½ miles, is recommended. The route is thus divided: Carrickfergus to Larne by road, 12 miles, but 14½ by rail, which is now open; Glenarm, 12; Cushendall, 13; to Ballycastle, 14½; to Giants Causeway (near Bushmills), 13 miles; inclusive of walking round Bellmore and Bengore Heads, when the grandest scenery presents itself. From Carrickfergus to Larne, you leave Glenoe valley on one side, and Larne Lough and Island Magee (belonging to the Donegal family) on the other. The cliffs and caves of the island are frequently basaltic, especially at the Gobbins. The new road begins at Larne, at a ledge, cut or blasted out of the cliff's side, a few feet above the sea, while the old road is 600 or 700 feet higher, and commands a view of the Scottish coast. Off Ballygally Head are the Maiden Rocks and Lights. Cairncastle, up the hills to the left, which are 1,000 to 1,200 feet high. *Glenarm*, the seat of the Earl of Antrim, head of the M'Donnels, on a beautiful bay at the mouth of a fine glen and a stream from Slemish Mountain (1,451 feet high), and which commands one of the most extensive views of open sea in the United Kingdom. Much lime and stone are sent to Scotland. Then come Straidkelly, Carn Lough (Colin Top to the left, 1,420 feet), Ringfadrock. *Drumnasole* (seat of A. Turnley, Esq., the owner,) is here. Nachore Mountain, 1,180 feet, Drumnaul Castle, on Garron Point, whence a noble sea view across to Scotland. Here the road turns to Glenariff, the finest of many picturesque glens opening into Red Bay, so called because of the colour of the sandstone cliffs. Past Clogh-i-Stookan Rock (curiously shaped), the Tunnel Rock and Caves, near Red Bay Castle, to Cushendall and its basalt pillars. Near this are Layde Church, her Ossian, they say, is buried, Court Martinrath, Lurg Eidem, and other haunts of Ossian's hero, Fin M'Coul, and Trosten Mountain, 1,800 feet high; then Castle Carey and Cushendern House and Bay. Proceeding over the desolate hills by the coast you come to Tor Point, near Cairnlea Mountain (1,250 feet) and Murlogh Bay, where the strata of the Ballycastle coal-field may be noticed – a mixture of coal, with clay, slate, shale sandstone, lime, and green basalt or whinstone. Coal is worked here.

Here the road turns off to Ballycastle, leaving Fair Head or Benmore Head to the right, a visit to which must on no account be omitted, as the basalt pillars exceed in beauty those of the Causeway. Boats may be obtained by going round Fair Head, if weather permit; but it may be examined, though not so well, by land. The vast basaltic mass is seen resting on an irregular base 300 feet thick, composed of the coal strata, above which it rises 336 feet higher, straight and solid as a wall, though found when examined to consist of jointed pillars packed closely together, some 20 to 30 feet across, and are, as geologists tell us, the 'work of internal firm'. Enormous blocks are heaped up round the base of the cliffs. A narrow chasm, called Gray Man's Path, cuts right through, and makes a rough sloping walk from the landward side down to the beach, with a glimpse of the sea; a broken pillar, like the shaft of a ruined temple, lies across it.

Opposite Fair Head, three or four miles distant, is Rathlin Island, with Bruce's Castle (where he found refuge), hanging over basaltic rocks resembling those on the main land. After Fair Head comes Salt Pans; then Ballycastle, an old seat of the M'Donnels, the Antrim family (the resemblance of the late lamented Earl to Charles the First was proverbially striking), whose burial-place is here, with the Abbey of Bonamargy, founded by them; and Kenbaan Castle, on a singular rock composed of chalk and basalt. The next thing is the famous Carrack-a-rede rock, which stands out 60 feet from the shore, to which it is joined only by a slender rope bridge across the chasm, 80 feet from the water. A fine view from the heights above it. Sheep Island, Ballintry, and Dunseverick Castle follow next, where the peculiar scenery round Bengore Head to Giant's Causeway begins; but the best plan is to go on to the Causeway Inn, at the other end or it, a few miles further on, where guides and boats may be hired. Guide, 2s 6d a day. It is usual to walk from here along the beach to Dunseverick, and then take the boat back, to obtain the full advantage of the effects. For four miles the coast is a series of little caves, rugged bays or ports, and picturesque rocks, most fancifully shaped, among which you walk, with a sort of undercliff on one side, several hundred feet high, composed of piles of basalt, mixed with ether rocks. Beginning at Port-na-baw, you pass Weir's Snoot, and the Great and Little Stoocans, two heap-like rocks, and turn into Port Gannixy. Then follow Aird's Snoot, and the Giant's Causeway, properly so called – consisting of a low promontory or rocky pier sloping into the sea for 800 or 900 feet, and made up of about 40,000 dark basalt

Above left: Fishermen going about their work at the Giant's Causeway in 1903. *(LoC) Above right*: The Causeway consists of around 40,000 interlocking basalt columns, shown here in close-up, which were formed by a volcanic eruption about fifty or sixty million years ago. *(Man vy) Below*: A view of the Giant's Causeway, c. 1895. *(LoC)*

pillars, tolerably upright and regular, mostly five or six sided, whilst some have only three, and others as many as nine sides. They are all jointed, and and 30 feet above the beach in the highest part, with an uneven surface 300 feet wide. Here they show Lord Antrim's parlour, the giant's gate, parlour, loom, theatre, etc.; then Port Noffer and Sea Gull rock, with the organ in the face of the cliffs, exactly like the pipes of an organ, the Dyke in Port Reostax: the Chimney Tops (thee or four solitary pillars over a corner of the cliff), leading into Port-na-Spania, where a ship of the Spanish Armada came ashore, and then another giant's organ in the cliffs. Then the Horse's Back and Port-na-Collian, which contains several strange rocks, as the Priest and his Flock, the Nursing Child, the King and his Nobles etc., Port-rea-Tobber and a second Sea-Gull island, then follow; the cliff above being called Lover's Leap. The next and grandest bay and fall is Port-na-Plaiskin, which should be seen from Hamilton's Seat, 400 feet above, so called from Dr Hamilton, whose interesting letters from the Northern Coast made the locality known to the world. The succession of pillars and stratifications of the rocks along this remarkable coast are now fully visible. Horse Shoe Harbour, Lion's Head (a red rock), Benbane Head, the Twins, Giant's Ball Alley, and Pulpit, follow next; then Bengore Head; the Giant's Granary and Four Sisters, in Port Fad; Contham Head leading round to Port Moon, which has a waterfall and a cave inside, Stack Rock, the Hen and Chickens, and other rocks, and at length Dunseverick Castle, built in the 12th century.

Westward of the Causeway, you may visit Port Coon Cave (100 yards long, into which boats can be rowed), the White Rocks, Priest's Hole Cave, and the remains of Dunluce Castle (formerly the M'Donnel's seat, on a wild rock cut off from the main land.

LONDONDERRY AND COLERAINE

This line skirts the east and south banks of Lough Foyle, an arm of the sea about 15 miles long and 10 broad, dividing the northern portion of Derry from that of the county of Donegal, and runs, via BELLARENA, MAGILLIGAN, etc., to

LONDONDERRY
A telegraph station. HOTELS – Imperial.
STEAMERS – See Bradshaw's Railway Guide.
MARKET DAYS – Wednesday, Thursday (flax), and Saturday.
FAIRS – June 17th, September 4th, October 17th.
BANKERS – Branch Bank of Ireland; Branch of Belfast Banking Company; Branch of Northern Banking Company, Branch of the Ulster Banking Company; Provincial Bank of Ireland.

The capital town of the county, which contains a population of about 35,529, who return one member. It stands on the western bank of the Foyle, and consists of

Enniskillen

Above: The Great Northern Railway's Enniskillen train, near Fintona Junction. *Below*: A colour view of the town looking across the River Erne. Enniskillen is located between the upper and lower sections of Lough Erne and its name is derived from *Inis Ceithleann*, meaning Ceithlenn's island. The GNR's line had linked the town with Derry from 1854, but it was closed by the government in 1957 and today the nearest station is at Sligo.

four principal streets, which cross each other at right angles, and from which a number of smaller ones diverge. As the ground on which the town is built is very hilly, many of the streets are exceedingly inconvenient for carriages, but every exertion has been made to repair this local disadvantage by the attention which is paid to the paving and lighting of them. The Cathedral is a very handsome edifice, built in the Gothic style of architecture. It was erected in 1633, and has, within the last few years, undergone extensive repairs. It has tombs of Doctors Knox and Hamilton, and two flags captured from the besiegers in May 1689. Farquhar, the poet, and Dr Hamilton were natives. Londonderry carries on a considerable commercial intercourse with America and the West Indies, It being favourably situated for commerce, and possesses an encellent secure harbour, with a splendid of quays. This place stood a siege of 105 days in 1688 against James II. The walls around the city are still in good preservation, forming a favourite promenade. Close to the city court house is a celebrated gun called 'Roaring Meg'. The bishop's palace, built in 1761 (the walls of which are 1,800 feet in circuit and 24 feet high) is a fine building.

DUNDALK, ENNISKILLEN, AND LONDONDERRY

Loudonderry to Enniskillen & Dundalk

CARRIGANS, close to which is *Dunmore*, the seat of R. M Criutock, Esq.

ST JOHNSTON, where fairs are held April 7th, October 13th, and November 26th.

PORTHALL station.

STRABANE has a population of about 6,000, principally employed in the linen trade. Markets held here on Tuesdays, and fairs first Thursday every month, May and November 12th. Close at hand are *Miltown*, Major Dumfries; *Hollyhill* and *Strabane Glen*, J. Sinclare, Esq.

SION MILLS and VICTORIA BRIDGE stations.

NEWTOWNSTEWART – This place was burnt by James II after the siege of Derry, but rebuilt in 1722: here is shown the house in which James II slept. Close at hand are King O'Nial's castle, in ruins, *Baron's Court*, Marquis of Abercorn; *Newtownstewart*, Hon. Major Crawford. Markets are held here on Mondays, and fairs monthly.

MOUNTJOY, close to which is the seat of C. J. Gardner, Esq.

Tyrone – A county in the province of Ulster, which returns two members, is bounded on the north by Londonderry, the south by Monaghan, the east by Loch-Neagh, and on the west by Donegal and Fermanagh. It is divided into four baronies.

OMAGH

A telegraph station. HOTEL – Harkness'.

MARKET DAY – Saturday. FAIRS – Monthly.

BANKERS – National Provincial Bank of Ireland; Ulster Banking Company.

Here are ruins of an Abbey founded in 792, Church, five Chapels, Market and Court House, Barracks, Reading Room, Hospital, etc.

FINTONA, where markets are held on Fridays, and Fairs the 22nd of every month, and close to which is *Ecclesville*, seat of C. Eccles, Esq.

DRUMORE ROAD, close to which is the town of Dromore, 'the Great Ridge', which has a population of about 14,954 employed in the linen trade; four chapels, market house, schools, clergy widows' houses, dispensary, factories, two bridges; on one of which there is a tablet to Bishop Percy; cathedral, built by Bishop Jeremy Taylor, whose tomb, together with that of Bishop Percy is here; Danish fort, remains of an elk, 10¼ feet between the horns. Fairs are held here on 1st Saturday in March, May 12th, August 6th, October 10th, December 14th; and Markets on Saturday for linen. Close at hand are *Gill Hall Castle*, Earl Clanwilliam; *Dromore House*, J. H. Quinn, Esq.

TRILLICK – Markets are held here for butter, on Tuesdays, and Fairs on the 14th of every month, and close by are the ruins of Castle Meragn.

IRVINGSTOWN ROAD, near to which is Lowtherstown, where Markets are held on the 8th of every month, and April 12th.

Fermanagh – This county, which returns two members, is divided by Lough Erne, which, properly speaking, consists of two lakes, the upper lake being nine miles in length, and from two to five in width, being connected with the former by a wide channel about seven miles long. The banks of these celebrated waters abound in picturesque scenes, although the surface of this county is not, in general, either productive or beautiful. Toward the northern division the land is tolerably productive, and farms are of considerable size. In other parts husbandry is more imperfectly understood.

BALLINAMALLARD station.

ENNISKILLEN

A telegraph station. HOTELS – Imperial.

MARKET DAY – Tuesday. FAIRS – 10th of every month (March excepted).

BANKERS – Branch of Belfast banking Company; Branch of Ulster Banking Company; National Provincial Bank of Ireland.

This town, which is situated in a fine spot on an island between Loughs Erne, contains a population of about 14,678, who are engaged in the corn and general trade, and returns one member. It has three chapels, court house, county prison, infirmary, town hall (in which are the banners taken at the battle of the Boyne), linen hall, school, cavalry and artillery barracks, two bridges, brewery, canneries, cutlery factory, Charles I's school, with ten exhibitions (five of £50 and £30). It is celebrated for the successful defence which the inhabitants made in 1688 on behalf of William III, and gives name to a regiment of dragoons. Close at hand are the beautiful seat and grounds of Lord Belmore, open to the public; *Florence Court*, Earl of Enniskillen; *Ely Lodge*, Marquis of Ely; *Tully Castle* and *Bellisle*, J. Porter, Esq.

LISBELLAW, MAGUIRE'S BRIDGE, LISNASKEA, and NEWTOWNBUTLER stations.

CLONES

A telegraph station. MARKET DAY – Thursday.

FAIRS – Last Thursday in every month.

This town contains a population of about 3,000, principally engaged in the linen manufacture. It has the remains of an abbey, founded by St Tierney. A connecting link is here formed between this line and the Midland Great Western, by which the Midland and more western districts are brought into much more intimate connection with those of the north. The line runs from Clones, via BELTURBERT, to Cavan, for continuation of the route to Galway.

Monaghan, which returns two members, is situated in the province of Ulster. Although this county is much incumbered with mountains and bogs, great portions of it are highly cultivated and improved (especially the northern parts). Numerous small lakes are in the country. The occupations of the population are chiefly agricultural , and the flax and turnip crops have of late been extensively cultivated. Agricultural and cattle shows are annually held, under the patronage of the country gentry. Large quantities of butter and other farm produce are sent to the English market.

NEWBLISS and MONAGHAN Road stations.

BALLYBAY – Here markets are held on Saturday, and Fairs on 3rd Saturday in every month. It is also the junction of the line to Cavan, 9 miles of which, to Cootehill are now open.

CASTLEBLANEY

A telegraph station. Telegraph station at Dundalk, 17¾ miles.

HOTEL – McMaster's. MARKET DAY – Wednesday.

FAIRS – 1st Wednesday in every month.

Castleblaney House, formerly belonging to Lord Blayney, has recently been purchased by Mr Hope, who has just put the beautiful grounds, spacious lake, etc., into exquisite order, and most liberally thrown them open to the public.

CULLOVILLE station.

Inniskeen was one of the chief seats of the Danes, and has ruins of several forts. Close at hand are *Northland*, Dean Adams; *Cabra Castle*, J. Pratt, Esq., close to the ruins of he old castle.

We now enter the county of Louth, and shortly after the town of...

Dundalk – see page 95.

Midland Great Western Railway poster for tours in Connemara, Galway, Achill and the west of Ireland, *c.* 1900.